QUIT COMPULSIVE GAMBLING

Quit
COMPULSIVE GAMBLING

The action plan for gamblers and their families

GORDON MOODY MBE

THORSONS PUBLISHING GROUP

First published 1990

Copyright © Gordon Moody 1990

British Library Cataloguing in Publication Data

Moody, Gordon
Quit compulsive gambling: the action plan for gamblers
and their families.
1. Families with gamblers. Self-help
I. Title
362.2'9

ISBN 0-7225-1601-0

Published by Thorsons Publishers Limited, Wellingborough, Northampton, NN8 2RQ, England

Typeset by Burns & Smith, Derby

Printed in Great Britain by Mackays of Chatham, Kent

1 3 5 7 9 10 8 6 4 2

Contents

Dedication

To my beloved wife Jess, without whose patient forbearance the work which made this book possible could never have been done.

Foreword

It was in 1964 that, in the course of three weeks, two patients who had attempted suicide for no apparent reason, were referred to me for treatment. On investigation, it eventually became apparent that in both cases there had been heavy gambling and the problems resulting from this had led to the suicide attempts. I had never come across this before and on talking to colleagues, apparently neither had they.

I searched the literature but could only find occasional brief references to gambling. It seemed that apart from the moral and the psychoanalytic approaches, there had been little interest in gambling as a cause of human behavioural problems. I felt sure that there were other dimensions. This was particularly so since casual observation demonstrated that a large number of licensed betting offices had suddenly appeared following the Betting and Gaming Act 1960. Also and rather paradoxically, although the law appeared to prohibit commercial gaming, there seemed to be a sudden mushrooming of gaming clubs. These, unlike the betting offices, appeared to offer odds which inevitably fleeced the punter.

I was perplexed. It was at this point that I heard that an organization called Gamblers Anonymous had held its first meeting in this country the previous week. I contacted them and it was suggested that I should meet Gordon Moody. When I did so, I was immediately struck by his humour and his compassion.

Shortly after this, I was approached by Gamblers Anonymous, which was about to start a second group in London. I was invited to become the group's Honorary Psychiatrist.

The first meeting I attended is indelibly imprinted on my mind. In the words of Gordon Moody, 'when I came through that door', I found that, 'in Gamblers Anonymous, there truly is a spell'. So it was that I would spend every Tuesday evening sitting in a smoke-filled room in Victoria, listening to 'the therapies'. It was not only an engaging, emotional experience, but it opened up to me a whole area of life that I never dreamt existed. For someone like myself who did not have a gambling problem, it was a revelation to listen to the stories recounted by the members. While they were full of human tragedy, they provided me with a tremendous insight, for which I shall always be grateful. Gordon Moody's book has vividly reawakened these early memories for me.

Fundamental to the organization was the personality of Gordon Moody. It was his energy and enthusiasm as well as his charm which took Gamblers Anonymous through its first few difficult years. Its growth and development is in no small part due to him.

It therefore gives me great pleasure to provide this Foreword to Gordon Moody's book. It is a unique and highly personalized account of the disorder that characterizes those who gamble excessively and the impact this has on their lives and those of their families. Gordon Moody also highlights the sad fact that, whereas in the past, the problem largely presented in mature men, now the disorder has percolated through to the youngest and most vulnerable members of our society.

However, the book does not confine itself to this but, in considerable detail, it demonstrates the healing effect of Gamblers Anonymous and its kindred organization of Gam-Anon. In addition, it highlights the support and comfort provided by Parents of Young Gamblers, a more recent organization which Gordon Moody also played a vital role in setting up.

It is a book that will give comfort and succour to those afflicted by excessive gambling; above all, it provides hope and light at the end of the tunnel. Only someone as steeped in the atmosphere of gambling and its impact, as Gordon Moody is, could have written this book.

In addition, people from the caring agencies will be provided not only with clear case histories, but also an insight into the predicament facing those who gamble excessively and cause problems to themselves and their families.

Quit Compulsive Gambling will aid those who fall prey to the disorder and inform those who wish to help them.

Dr Emanuel Moran FRCP FRCPsych
Chairman, The National Council on Gambling
Senior Consultant Psychiatrist, Chase Farm Hospital

Preface

What you need to know before you read on

First, apart from general readers who, I hope, will enjoy it, this book is especially intended for:

- The families and friends of those whom we call compulsive or addicted gamblers. Here they can read that their situation is understood, that it is not unique, that there is hope and help and something they can do.

- Members of what are generally known as the 'helping professions' or the 'caring agencies'. I hope that my description of the onset of this problem, its development, effects and control will assist them to recognize, understand and help those of their patients or clients who are, or are related to, compulsive gamblers.

- Those gamblers themselves. They are not likely to read or make sense of this book while they are still gambling, but, in recovery, it may help them understand what happened to them while they were gambling and what is happening to them now.

Second, I have written from personal experience. I have learned about these things from Gamblers Anonymous and Gam-Anon in the course of 24 years' intimate 'family' relationship. What I have heard, seen and pondered imaginatively I now pass on to you.

Third, two significant circumstantial changes have occurred during those 24 years. They are dealt with in chapters 11 and 12. You may wonder why they were not absorbed into the account given in the earlier chapters. The reason is that the shape and substance of that account was determined by my deepest impressions which were formed in the first few years of my involvement, when it was most intense. In any case, though, there has been no essential change. People whose circumstances differ still recognize the same fundamental experience in each others' lives.

Fourth, I have written enthusiastically. I don't think I have exaggerated the problems faced by gamblers and their families, nor, I believe, have I exaggerated the sense of release, relief and joy their new life brings. I may have made the process of recovery seem more easy, more inevitable, than it is. If I have, it is because the whole experience has, for me, been so exciting, so wonderful – a sort of magical transformation of people's lives, making them new. Remember, too, that I have been an involved spectator. I have lent a hand, advised sometimes, always encouraged, but I have seen it happen. From such a viewpoint, and about such a prospect, one must wax lyrical. Those who feel they must, will, I think, be able to interpret what I say in their own professional or academic terminology.

Fifth, this experience necessarily came to me by accident, I could not have planned it. Indeed, I did not expect anything like it to happen when, in 1958, I became Secretary of the Churches' Council on Gambling in the UK – my introduction to the subject. I moved in the right direction, I believe, when I decided to try to understand the attraction gambling holds, rather than to pursue the moral issue. I learned a good deal, as, from time to time, I visited greyhound tracks, race courses, betting offices and bingo clubs, talking whenever I could with their owners or managers. What surprised and impressed me most was that some of those people I met appeared (as I put it to myself) to be 'stuck' with gambling and that it was doing them no good. When I read in the Press that an organization called Gamblers Anonymous existed in the United States of America, I believed that we needed it here too, yet I was powerless to do anything about it. Then on 27th May 1964, after I had addressed a meeting at the South Croydon Methodist Church on the subject of gambling, a man, accompanied by his wife, approached me. He said, 'I am a compulsive gambler and a member of Gamblers Anonymous.' They were Henry and Vivian F of a GA group based in Brooklyn, New York. You will meet them again later in the book. I replied, 'Let's get going.'

In the weeks that followed they taught me a great deal, enough for me to understand – and to be understood by – anyone seeking help with the problem. I found rooms for the meetings in Dawson House, Tufton Street, Westminster, the rear premises of the Abbey Community Centre, which has its front entrance in Marsham Street. In consultation with Henry and Vivian, I prepared a Press release and called a Press conference for the 7th July. Because there was no alternative, I gave the Churches' Council's address and telephone number for those who wished to make contact.

There was a good attendance at the conference. I briefly introduced Henry who told of his gambling years and of his time in Gamblers Anonymous. Many questions followed and, in all, we were there for an hour and a half.

The following morning, every national daily carried a prominent and helpful account of the proceedings. When I arrived in my office, the telephone was ringing and throughout that day, it was not quiet for more than a few seconds at a time. I felt as though I had taken the lid off a cauldron I did not previously know had existed. It was scarcely easier the next two days. We soon learned to answer simply: 'Abbey 4252'. From the first sentence, we knew if the caller wanted the Council or Gamblers Anonymous.

Here I must pay tribute to my secretary, the late Lilian Tarbath. Born before the First World War, she was a gently and protectively nurtured only child, who had been brought up to think no good of gambling or gamblers. Yet she took it all in her stride. Over the next seven years until she retired, she talked many into going to Gamblers Anonymous and Gam-Anon. She was proud to be known as GA Lil, providing coffee and biscuits to enquirers and to members of Gamblers Anonymous who liked having a drop-in headquarters. She got to know those who were taxi drivers very well!

On the evening of 10 July, Henry and Vivian called for me, and we went to Dawson House. We found ten men and two women in the Gamblers Anonymous room and two women in the Gam-Anon room. Both meetings were successful. More wives attended the second week and, as time passed, the numbers in both rooms steadily increased.

Henry took the chair in the Gamblers Anonymous room, sitting between Dr Ronald Casson and myself. Dr Casson, a group therapist who was interested in addictions, had come at my invitation. Henry had told me that many groups liked to be in touch with a psychiatrist. For eleven years he attended the Friday meeting, speaking as rarely as I did, but being prepared to talk to members afterwards, and several consulted him privately. Sadly, he died following a heart attack in 1975. His association with the group was not typical. Normally, only members attended closed meetings, but groups are free to make any arrangements they want.

When I first met Henry and Vivian I expected that my involvement would end once the Press conference was over. Using the Council's telephone number changed all that and, in any case,

I knew from the first evening that I had become part of it all. I attended meetings regularly often more than once a week as the movement spread. The correspondence, telephone calls and visitors to the office more than filled my already-busy days. For a few years, I attended all committee meetings, local and national. I enjoyed sharing in what I can only call exciting exploits as we went here and there in the attempt to establish new groups.

Henry's period of service for his company in London ended in January 1965 and he and Vivian returned to the United States. Both were much missed, but they had laid the foundations and prepared people to take office so well that the meetings did not falter. Soon afterwards, Gamblers Anonymous made Dr Casson Honorary Psychiatrist and myself Honorary Founder-Patron for the UK.

When, in 1971, the Churches' Council, short of funds, closed the Westminster office and moved the work to my home in Berkshire, Gamblers Anonymous secured an address from which letters could be collected and a telephone which could be transferred to the homes of other members by day and night. From that time, my activities were reduced, although I attended London meetings frequently and others in various parts of the country from time to time until my retirement in 1978. Since then, my principal connection has been through the Gamblers Anonymous General Services Board, of which I was Chairman from its inauguration in 1975 until June 1988.

It was my intention to include a brief history of Gamblers Anonymous somewhere in the book but lack of space has precluded that. However, readers are given an adequate introduction to the life and activities of Gamblers Anonymous and Gam-Anon. Parents of Young Gamblers was launched in the UK in July 1986. For some years I had been aware that many parents needed such an organization to find each other and knew that I must do something about it. The opportunity came when I met the parents of a teenage gambler who lived near me and who was ready to take sustained action. The breakthrough came when we met Richard Murphy of the Spectrum Childrens' Trust. He offered us the use of the Trust's office in Taunton thereby providing Parents of Young Gamblers with the launching pad and headquarters which it needed.

Finally, I am grateful to those who read various chapters before the text was finalized. Denise Cullington, a clinical psychologist, made comments and posed questions on the first nine chapters and stirred me to explain myself more clearly in a number of places. Most of the book was read by a member of Gamblers Anonymous and a member of Gam-Anon while it was in its early stages. I am indebted to them for their help and valuable encouragement. Chapter 12 was improved considerably as a result of observations made by the mother of a young gambler. Chapter 13, where we read of Gordon House, was read there and apparently passed muster. Still, I alone am responsible for the whole, and it must bear the strengths and weaknesses of being based on personal experience. I hope it will help some of those who are in deep distress to find the 'normal way of thinking and living' they so desperately need.

People you must meet before you read on

He had worked all day and into the night. Now it was after midnight. His pockets were empty. He was cold, hungry and miserable. He pulled his taxi to the kerb, stopped, got out, and looked about listlessly. He was a pathetic sight. It was not surprising that a passing tramp asked him if he would like some soup. He went along and joined a group of derelicts on the embankment. 'Why am I here?' he asked himself. He was not like these people — he had a bed, a home and a wife. He knew the answer, he had 'gone down' again, like thousands of his bets, including those at the club tonight.

* * * * *

She was hungry, and so were her children. She heard her two teenage daughters talking as they looked at what little bread was left in the cupboard. One said to the other, 'The two little ones need it more than we do.' Their father was in regular, well-paid work, but it was often like this – he was a gambler.

* * * * *

He opened the case eagerly. He was really looking forward to playing the new electric guitar his aunt had given him. He reached inside and suddenly felt sick and angry as he found his old guitar. He knew what had happened – his brother had sold the new one for a pittance for money to play the machines in the arcades and shops. It had been like this for five years, since his brother was thirteen. Nothing in the house, especially money, was safe. No one knew what might happen next, it was like constantly living on the edge of a volcano. His brother was a gambler.

* * * * *

She hastily gave her children an apology for a meal, hurried them off to bed and prepared something better for her husband. As he ate it, she lied, saying she had eaten with the children. It was as well he did not ask too many questions, she had so much to hide, especially the debts. They scared her. She told herself it wasn't the bingo – she could afford that, and sometimes she won. No, it was the machines at the bingo club. All the money she won, all she skimped elsewhere, including the money for the bills, went on them. It was driving her insane but she couldn't stop.

1
Is there a gambler in the house?

If someone in your family were to gamble excessively, like the people you have just read about, how would you know? What would you see? One thing is sure, you would have no clear view of the gambling. Indeed, for a long time you might not even suspect it. When you did, it might take you a long time to prove that gambling rather than anything else was the root of the trouble.

Yes, the root of the *trouble*, for there would be trouble, and you would be worried about that person. It is equally certain that your worry would not be clear and straightforward. Many things would be wrong but there would be no clear pattern. The last person to help you get to the bottom of it would be the person you were worried about. He or she would be a past master (or mistress) at explaining everything away. It might be he, or she, but it is far more likely to be a father, husband, son or brother than a mother, wife, daughter or sister. Since 1964, the overwhelming majority of members of Gamblers Anonymous have been men and it is still unusual to see a woman in a group. There are now many boys, but hardly any girls. For that reason, I shall refer to the gambler as *he* and *him* throughout the principal chapters, and indicate the differences that occur when women gamble in chapter 10. The difference it makes when children gamble will be dealt with in chapter 12. This chapter, therefore, is addressed to the wife or partner of a gambler. Even so, I am sure that those whose concern is for a woman or girl or boy gambler will equally be able to recognize their basic experience here.

When did it start?

The gambling probably started before marriage. Many wives said that they knew their husbands gambled but they didn't realize how serious it was. One said that before her marriage she regarded her fiancé's continual money crises as small weaknesses which a steady marriage could cure. How wrong she found herself to be!

The gambling may start after marriage. If so, you will see a change of performance, personality and even appearance. The transformation is never, perhaps, complete, at least not for a long time. People think of Jekyll and Hyde – the happier, more loving, more caring person you once knew surfaces sometimes, and still seems, in spite of everything, to be the real one.

What happens?

You will experience doubt and uncertainty, recurring worries and perplexities, with intermittent waves of reassurance. The gambler becomes like a hero of one of those films about men engaged on secret war-time missions or involved in espionage. They are unable to explain their erratic movements which disrupt the family life and so their families begin to doubt and become suspicious. The *known* person is no longer reliably *there*, he becomes secretive, elusive, has to say 'trust me' over and over again, and consequently breeds yet more distrust.

The same thing happens to gamblers. Although they are physically near, they tend to withdraw into themselves. They become lost in their own thoughts and when questioned, they are likely to become evasive and impatient. They develop a secret life and there are money problems – many wives suspect that there is another woman. Quite frequently, as problems increase, gamblers take to drinking heavily, and that may be blamed. This change in personality is likely to give you the sharpest and deepest pain – having someone, yet not having them; knowing someone, yet not knowing them; wanting to trust, but not being able to do so.

It is clear that something holds this person in its grasp, but you do not know what it is. You can see it envelop him. There are problems about time. He slips out to buy a paper and does not return for hours. When he does come back, there is a story about meeting an old friend. It seems bizarre, but it is not altogether unbelievable. It is strange how often he is delayed at work or on the way home. You want to believe it all, and you do, for as long as you can, but a little maggot of disbelief works away in your mind. Your trust is undermined, in spite of yourself.

There are also problems about money. He earns a regular income, but there is never any money. Perhaps he is financially accident-prone: some or all of it has been lost or he has been robbed, or there was an error in his pay or the money for the wages was not collected from the bank. Often there are unexpected expenses with the car and sometimes friends need a loan – there is always an explanation. It is given convincingly, yet somehow it does not convince. The cumulative effect of all this is to leave you feeling lost in a fog with no clear idea where you are.

The next thing that happens is that things begin to disappear from the home. The lawnmower has been borrowed by a friend, or so he says – at any rate it isn't returned. Things you value, that you thought you both valued, also vanish. Your own possessions, and the money from your purse start to go as well. Your husband either knows nothing about it, or he has an explanation for its disappearance. He may spend hours helping you search for it, knowing full well what has really happened. He will manipulate you, making you doubt your own reliability. Are you really careless? Can you have mislaid or lost all those things?

How does it affect your friends and family?

Difficulties start to arise with your family and friends. Friends become more distant. You do not know it, but he has been borrowing from them and not repaying the money. You tend to become more and more isolated. It is not just that you sense a change in others, there is a change in you too. There is so much that you cannot speak of to anyone. Normally, we find relief in talking about our troubles. This, however, is intangible, shameful, and your shame, in a way, is as much as his, perhaps greater.

You will be driven to confrontation, to humiliating rows, suffering passions and feelings of which you never thought you were capable. You begin to wonder what sort of person you are. You feel unclean, you dislike and despise yourself. The confrontations are useless, he just retreats behind an iron curtain, a change comes over his eyes. Usually, we use our eyes to communicate with each other but your gambler hides behind his, especially when he is 'explaining' something. There is no discussion, it is a matter of take it or leave it. A denial and an explanation become much the same thing. If you persist there will be a row. He will create it but your fuse is short and you will play your part. It will be a relief to you, a distressing, humiliating relief, like scratching an itch and creating a sore. When he takes advantage of this, blames you for the whole thing and stamps out of the house, he leaves you feeling guilty as well as ashamed.

Those uncommunicating eyes are more and more contained in an

uncommunicative body. He sits around the house absorbed. He
pretends to read the paper or watch the television. It looks as though
he wants to ignore and be ignored. He can become angry if disturbed. He seems sullen, superior, disapproving, miserable – your reading
of his mind is probably determined by the way you feel at the time.

If there are other people in the house, particularly if there are
young children, they suffer too. A mother, frustrated and tormented
by her husband, tends to take it out on her children, and quite il-
logically and unjustly puts them in the wrong. That is not absolutely
exceptional. Parents generally tend to do this when they are aggrieved with each other, with other people or with life and when they
can find no relief or redress. But the gambler's wife finds herself doing it as a regular thing. It is another way to scratch an itch and create
a sore. It is another route to humiliation, shame, guilt and loss of
self-respect.

Add to all this the burden of struggling to make far too distant
ends meet, worrying about where the food is to come from, seeing
the children and yourself shabbily clad and insufficiently protected
from the weather, realizing that your neglected home is itself in
danger if the rent is not paid or the mortgage kept up, trying with
what shreds of pride are left to keep all this from the prying eyes that
you feel are turned on you, and it is clear that this is a disintegrating
and demoralizing experience. The capacity to think clearly and act
decisively is eroded away.

From time to time you need help, perhaps from the doctor or
social services, but you will not mention gambling, even if you
suspect or know for certain that it is the cause of the trouble. Because
you do not mention gambling your story seems lame, even to you.
To others it appears that you are covering something up. Your husband, on the other hand, if he is there or has to be interviewed,
somehow manages to be alert and engaging and wins sympathy for
having so useless a wife. You half believe that this is true, and search
yourself for ways in which you have failed and let him down, driving
him to all this.

There is more to come, though. Although he is by nature a bright
and energetic person, capable of getting and holding down a good
job and earning a good salary or running his own business, his work,
inevitably, suffers. Ultimately he may lose his job or his business will
go bankrupt, but before that he will have his first crisis.

This crisis puts him under tremendous pressure, which affects you
and all around you. You feel the pressure, it dominates him and it
dominates you. He has no mercy. He foists the problem on anyone

he thinks will respond with money. He names a sum and says that if it is not found immediately he will go to prison or the family will be thrown out of the house. You are terrified and, before you know where you are, you are colluding with him, helping him get the family together and pleading with them to save him or the home for you and the children. Afterwards, you realize the extent of your collusion and, especially when you discover that he is *still* gambling, you feel even more ashamed.

As well as these major crises there are continual smaller shocks. Bills he swore he had paid prove not to have been paid; letters from banks and building societies reveal desperate situations. People you have never seen before come to the door for him and some threaten you about debts. There is an explanation every time, plausible if not adequate, but, when they are put together, they create only doubt and confusion in you and, in the end, total, angry disbelief.

The debt remains a threat however, and the wife who never finds herself working or borrowing to clear it is either very strong or very lucky. Eventually the wife becomes as involved as her husband in the consequences of his gambling. Her life is conditioned by what he is and does. She responds to his Jekyll moments with relief, if also with suspicion. She reacts violently to his Hyde manifestations, as each time he becomes more and more abusive. She twists and turns to stay alive, learns to hate as well as despise him, and becomes bitter.

She cannot help that. It has her in its grip. One such woman, as Sunday after Sunday she received Holy Communion, prayed earnestly that God would take the hatred and bitterness from her heart. She hated the burden of it, but it was still there as she made her way home.

There can be no peace, no relaxation, not even when he is away from home all evening, all night, all weekend, even for a week or more at a time. If it is just a night or a weekend she is worrying about how much he has lost this time, what new crisis he will bring home. If it lengthens into a week, extraordinary though it may seem, she becomes concerned about him because she knows his desperation has taken him to the edge of crime, if not into it. She may already have followed him to court and visited him in prison. At the least, he is probably wandering somewhere and sleeping rough. The second time it happens, she knows he will return weary, dirty and desperate, and that she will look after him.

Why doesn't she leave him?

Some wives do leave their gambling husbands, of course, and the tendency to do so is increasing. That aspect of the matter is discussed further in chapter 11. But the burdens and bewilderment which are all part of the experience tend to erode the ability to make decisions. In such circumstances people tend to feel numbed and lifeless and just drag on from day to day.

When first she realized she had a problem, it was outside her. It was another person, her husband. Now her problem is inside her. Indeed, she is her own insoluble problem. She is all tangled up, she cannot find even one loose end from which to unravel it all. She can only go round its twists and turns, thinking she will go mad in the process.

She may no longer hope for it, but there *is* relief. More than an escape route, there is somewhere to go. There is rest and healing for her tortured mind. That, however, is for chapter 5. In the meantime, there are other questions to answer.

How will you know you have a gambler in the family?

You will have a persistent but indefinite worry about that person. Their personality will undergo a change and they will start to develop a secret life. Their new Jekyll and Hyde character will sow the seeds of doubt and uncertainty in your mind.

They will take to isolating themselves from friends and from familiy. They will pressurize you for money as they begin to experience financial problems.

Money and possessions will begin to disappear from the house. You will be put off if you ask for explanations and any explanations given will be given convincingly but will not actually convince. Direct questions will evoke denials; in themselves many explanations equal denials. There will be passionate confrontations which you will hate.

The gambler's work and general living standards will steadily suffer. When they are away from home you will fear for their safety and worry about whether or not they have become involved in crime.

2

The inside story

What is this gambling like for the gambler? At first, it is a wonderful new experience, like making a great discovery or falling in love. One man, recovering from this fatal infatuation, referred to his 'love affair with Lady Luck'. It begins with a whole-hearted response to 'action' gambling. This is no odd flutter or little game. The enjoyment of the 'action' is enjoyment of taking risk after risk in rapid and continuous succession, and risk really *means* risk – you catch your breath when you realize what is at stake.

This experience provides a door to a magical new world. It is amazing: there you are, engrossed at a gaming table, in a betting office or face-to-face with a gaming machine, lost to all the world. From the outside it looks so cramping, so limited, but you are experiencing the magic of Dr Who's Tardis. For the person who is in on the 'action' it is like the whole universe, bright with stars and full of wonder. At first it is all pure and innocent, the sheer zenith of the enjoyment of play.

Some people will find that hard to believe. Gambling is generally regarded as a negative activity. If you are ready to appreciate its positive appeal, cast your mind back to the games of chance you played in your childhood, or watch your children or grandchildren. Playing with chance is exhilarating and captivating. Perhaps no activity, engaged in for no extrinsic purpose, can quicken the pulse and concentrate attention so immediately or to so great an extent. When stakes are added, you play with risk as well as with chance. For that reason, gambling, especially 'action' gambling, is not for everyone, any more than any other form of risk taking is for everyone. Indeed, most people do no more than dabble in it – what appears to be the peak of life for one leads to fear in the pit of the stomach for another. If gambling really appeals to you you recognize that at once. You see that gambling separates the men from the boys, you stand taller than ordinary punters, you are Jack the Lad, a Big Shot. The 'action' makes you feel good and will go on doing so even when your life is falling to pieces around you.

You *must* go back and get more. For a while, the innocence and purity remain untouched. You are using time and money normally devoted to other things, but at first you can afford it and are neglecting only other leisure pursuits. You are not thinking of that, though, only enjoying your new life to the full.

All too soon, however, gambling begins to trespass onto areas of your life where it has no right to be. You start to rob your family of time and perhaps take some money from your savings. No one else may notice the first, and certainly no one will know about the second, but *you* are aware of both. You have to give *yourself* an explanation, because part of you demurs. Why are you devoting that time and money to gambling? Well, you are a good husband and father, you do your job well, work hard, get a good income, look after them at home, so surely you have a right to some enjoyment of your own. The money from your savings will not be missed, and can be replaced; no one will suffer. This, however, is the beginning of that deviousness which, though it sets you free to gamble, will, eventually, make you a slave.

Still, you do not consider the consequences, you have hushed your conscience for the time being. All you know is that you have to get back to the 'action', and for that you need both time and money. It is no use arguing or asking questions.

Over the weeks and months, it becomes more and more serious. You look again at the balance of the savings account, it is always going down. There is not much left, and nothing is being put back, but you *will* win it back. You remember winning runs, some lasting several days. Next time that happens, you will put back all you have taken and still have some money for gambling. You conveniently forget that, most of the time, your winnings are your secret gambling money, none even going on a present for the family. Deep down, though, you know there is no real winning. Wherever you find the 'action', the odds are against you and, win or lose, you must keep going until either the 'action' stops or you run out of money. If that fact of your new life cannot be forgotten it has to be suppressed, because the 'action' is compelling and you must have it, whatever the cost. You are now deceiving yourself, excellent practice in the art that will become so essential to your gambling career, that of deceiver and confidence trickster. The innocence and purity are gone.

The savings account is now empty. It is no longer something no one *will* know about, it has become something no one *must* know about. At home, you pretend, acting as if all is well. You must deceive your family, too, act your part. Having practised so much on yourself, it is not too difficult. You have a vivid imagination and have developed it to the point that you are now living in a dream world. You have created your own reality, your own priorities, your own right and wrong. It is not difficult, therefore, to justify stealing from your home, to find reasons for household economies, to explain why there is no longer as much money as there was, to explain empty or reduced pay packets, to borrow outside the home, to take up a second mortgage, to persuade the bank manager that you need a loan, to get money anywhere you can.

None of this was intended. You are not a bad man, in a way, you are not even a liar. It just seemed inevitable as, indeed, once you are captivated in this way by gambling, it is. None the less, by degrees, you have been corrupted. You are now under pressure: friends and acquaintances want their money back; your relatives and your wife's relatives, who in the past have helped you out of 'difficulties', now view you in a different light. The bank and the building society want payments on their loans. Above all, you still want more money for gambling so you borrow at higher interest. This is pressure indeed, and pressure is exactly what you cannot stand. Along with your powerful dream world imagination, you have above-average impatience. This has played its part from the beginning. A bank official of young middle age explained the start of it as follows:

> *You have three bills to pay but money enough for one. You play that up to win the money for the three, but you only lose. A friend lends you money: now you can either pay the bills or pay him, so you play that money up to get enough to settle both debts, and you lose again.*

So the problems spiral. Patience and prudence would have avoided all that but for you impatience makes prudence impossible and the dream world your imagination creates offers the certainty of a win, removing all sense of danger. Once you have progressed to raising money like this you inevitably build up enough trouble for some of it to come to the surface. You never know when you are likely to be confronted by creditors at home, at work, or in the street. You are always on your guard, you avoid certain streets at certain times but if a creditor does catch you, you meet them with a smile and say:

'I am sorry. I had the money ready on Monday as I promised, but our son had an accident on the way to school. He is getting on all right, but his clothes were torn and I had to use the money to get new ones. You know how expensive they are. I hope you can hang on. I will come and see you next Monday.'

There's a story, just like that, straight off, without preparation. That's your dream world for you. He sympathizes, hopes the boy will be better quite soon and gives you more time than you asked for. You lap up the sympathy. You need it, there is precious little of it at home. There are confrontations. Things are too far out of joint for anyone not to notice or to accept it all without question. Everything comes down to money and time. Where were you and where is the money? Explanations still come readily – they may not satisfy anyone, but at least they stop the questions and get you out of what you regard as a trap. If the questions persist, you can be very hurt that your honesty is doubted.

For a long time you do not mention gambling. They probably know you gamble, but, if they have no experience of anything like this, it would never occur to them that anyone could lose all that money and all that time on gambling. You are very careful though. You get up early and are first to get to the post. You may even meet the postman in the street. You make sure you take all the telephone calls and, if others are present, have some extraordinary conversations, talking about anything under the sun while a baffled creditor is trying to bring the conversation round to the payment of a debt.

It is all a nightmare, of course, but you take each difficulty as it comes, ducking one, skirting round another, always pursuing your goal: getting back to gambling. You have such resilience! You live through days it would exhaust most other people even to hear about.

This is a perilous way of living. You are like a man desperately trying to keep his balance on the crazily moving platform of gambling, while at the same time attempting an impossible feat of juggling. But instead of plates, you are trying to keep your family life, your home, your job, your solvency and the rags of your reputation and credibility in the air.

Cracks begin to appear in your façade. Final demands for payment get through to the family and bank statements are eventually seen; a creditor calls at the door or telephones while you are out. Your audience becomes more and more stony but it is remarkable how amazed you can be at the stupidity of the rest of the world. Of course, you have paid the bills and of course, there is money in the bank. People make such a muddle of things. You may not convince anybody but for now you evade capture. However, a rift has developed between you and your family. A war is on, a guerilla war. One of movement, surprise and attrition. Friends are going or gone, and your wife's relatives have given up on you. You do not mind: you don't need them, never did think much of them in fact. Members of your family tend to avoid contact with you. Your own parents, though perhaps not your brothers and sisters, may still cling to the hope that all will be well, and from time to time they pay dearly for this.

About this time you experience your first crisis. Until now, having had a wide area of manoeuvre you have managed to sort out a problem in one quarter by raising money in another. You have kept some sources sweet by paying part of a debt out of your winnings so that you can go back again for more. Now, however, you need to get out of trouble quickly, and cannot manage it in your usual way, but the situation still has to be resolved. Once people start catching up with you, where will it end? You will be overwhelmed.

So you resort to the family, the more of them the better, parents and in-laws included. They will come to your rescue for your wife's and children's sake. You manage wonderfully. Having successfully thrown the problem in their laps, as we described in the previous chapter, you become all charm and humility. You confess to as much of the gambling as you need to get what you want. Your manner is submissive, your voice and eyes low. You have learned your lesson you say and will never gamble again. You swear to that, on the Bible, your mother's life, your child's life. Anything, so long as you get the money. But you *will* gamble again and as soon as you can. If your plan has worked you will have added some stake money to the amount you needed to clear the debt.

How could anyone I know and love sink so low?

Is he just a deceiver, manipulating friends and family without mercy and chuckling over it afterwards? Certainly he is a deceiver, a manipulator and merciless. He also knows what he is doing and why he is doing it. If your only interest is to judge him, bother with him no more, just leave him to his fate.

But I think you would like to understand him, and learn why and how his character and personality are so changed. The fact is that he has chosen new goals, and to achieve them he has to follow new paths. In doing this he has 'put on', like a coat, a different 'person'. If (and when) he stops gambling and recovers, he will take that 'person' off again (a harder process) and be himself once more.

In the meantime, gambling dominates him. That crisis had to be resolved so that he could carry on. In any case, he has by this time become largely insensitive to people. Even his wife and children signify in his life only as means to serve his ends, or as hindrances to his purposes.

We have not yet gone into detail about the ways he has misused and abused other people. Perhaps there is no need, those who suffer living with or near this kind of gambler will find endless instances racing through their minds. For others, one illustration may be enough. His daughter was just eight years old. She had received some money for her birthday and proudly put it into her new Post Office Bank account. Her mother hoped it would be safe there. At eight years old, she had to make withdrawals personally. Her father asked her if she would like to help Daddy. Of course, she would, so off they went, hand in hand. She withdrew the money and gave it to him. He took her home and went straight on to the betting office. It all went down on the first race. Any father of a trusting daughter will understand his mortification, that he felt he could have killed the bookmaker, destroyed the betting office and killed himself. He did not do any of that, however, nor did he stop gambling or change himself, because he *could* not. Gamblers work off such emotions by shouting, being offensive, banging and smashing things, by fighting or by striking out at their wives or children. It may or may not relieve their frustration, but it certainly deepens their degradation and self-loathing. Self-respect has long since vanished.

At home, he is a stranger. Trapped in a family gathering, he will be oblivious to all that is going on. His foot, absentmindedly but obediently tapping out the rhythm, will show that he is aware of music, but that is all. He is trying to work his problems out. But he will never work them out until he wakes up to the truth of things. In his mind they go round and round.

Each morning he wakes up wondering where to get the money for today's gambling. He has a map in his head that shows where treasure may be found. He runs up and down its paths, finding this treasure trove worked out, that one too dangerous to approach. Then he sees a spot he has not visited lately or had not noticed before. Life returns, impatience gives him energy and the dream world builds his confidence. This will be a pushover. Someone had better watch out, a master confidence trickster is coming.

You may wonder how he can recover confidence so soon after the losses and humiliations of the day before. The dream world sees to that. One man, as he often did, lost everything at the greyhounds and emerged into a cold, wet night, with no money for the bus journey home. He climbed into bed in a miserable state. As he warmed up and became more comfortable his mind went back to the track. He looked over the card again, studying the 'form' of the various dogs. He could see it now – those dogs had to win. How could he have missed it? He decided on a stake, went through the programme race by race, winning all the time. He knew the odds at which each dog had won. Each time he knew just what he collected and each time it all went on the next race. He saw himself driving a new expensive car, he was so happy. Then he became aware of his wife, sleeping beside him. How mean of him to leave her out of it! He started again, increasing his first stake. Again he went triumphantly through the programme and there she was, beside him in the car, dressed in the best fur coat that money could buy. As he dropped into a contented sleep he *knew* that that's how it would be tomorrow and then they would live happily ever after. After all, he was a good gambler, even a great one, perhaps the best, though unlucky sometimes. So he was prepared for the next day's 'action'.

He is absolutely committed now. Like Macbeth he is in so far that to go back would be as far as to go right over – indeed further. To get right over he needs only that final, debt-clearing, fortune-making win or succession of wins. To go back, he would have to settle all those debts one by one and, whatever his annual income, they will equal it several times over. There is a sliding scale, the greater the income, the greater the debts. In any case, there is his family. They despise him; some of them hate him. He must convince them by that big win that he was right all the time.

His dream world also enables him to believe that he, not the family, is the injured party. If they do not co-operate with him he can feel aggrieved. One gambler's wife borrowed £1,000 in her own name to clear some of her husband's debts and took a job on the London buses to pay it back. Her life was hard, but one day, when she was collecting fares at the front of the lower deck in the rush hour, he jumped on to the step and called, in his great voice, for her to give him five pounds. She was confused and embarrassed, but she refused. As he dropped off, he cried, 'What sort of a wife do you think you are?' What sort of a husband *he* was, it did not occur to him to think.

Another man, looking back on his wasted years, recalled how his world had been filled with 'bastards'. The owners, trainers, jockeys of losing horses, the owners and trainers of losing greyhounds, bookmakers, people who would not lend him money, those who wanted their money back, they were all 'bastards'. Now he knew that *he* had been the 'bastard', but he could not see it then. Had he done so he would have been lost. He could stay on his feet only if he stayed in motion.

What a state of mind! Gnawed by guilt, harried by problems, the victim of intense aggravation when things go against him, he experiences the deep loneliness of the rejected. He rebels against the world which excludes him. He despises as dull those who do not gamble, and their silly treadmill of work and family life. He is wracked and torn beyond belief. For a long while, perhaps all through his gambling career, he still loves gambling, but its meaning changes. Increasingly, it has negative features; it becomes a place of escape, not from his creditors, but from himself. While he is gambling, his dream world dominates – he is king again, but no longer in the same way. Now, the shadows of his problems, the sense of impending ruin, his guilt, all pursue him there. He may not even be able to stay in the betting office to hear the result of the race on which he has bet. His stomach is working so much that he feels sick. He may drive to another betting office and read the result on the board there.

He is a sorry sight. He spends nothing on clothes, and he does not care for those he has. He does not eat enough. He does not care what people think of him. He keeps going because he must. He tells himself he has to gamble his way out of the problems he has gambled himself into. He slips into crime. He prepared himself for this by making cynical use of family, friends, workmates and acquaintances, stealing as well as borrowing from them. The person he once was, and can become again, would have done none of this. His crimes are such as he has opportunity to commit, petty theft, burglary, embezzlement, small or large scale fraud, and confidence tricks. His obsession drives him through it all. His crimes, like everything else, are committed 'under the influence' of gambling. He tells himself he is only borrowing the money, that when he wins he will put it back and, in his confused way, he believes it.

He may or may not escape discovery. He may go to court, be put on probation, be fined, or sent to prison. The world will expect him to 'learn his lesson'. In a way he does, but fruitlessly. One man who came out of prison three times said, 'You resolve never to bet again, and you don't – until the time of the first race.'

It all has to end somewhere. A fair proportion of those you see sleeping rough or gathering round the doors of hostels are gamblers of this kind. They have lost their jobs, their families, and their homes. Perhaps they walked out, perhaps they were shown the door. Does it matter which? You will meet some more in chapter 13. They are not necessarily a permanent population. One man, when he could not face his wife, used to sleep on Aldgate Underground Station in London. The head of the mathematics department of a London comprehensive school wandered behind hotels in Bristol, picking scraps to eat from the waste bins, while his wife and small daughter were being evicted and taken to a hostel for the homeless. Afterwards they set up home together again.

One evening, a recovering gambler and I went to a meeting together. He had risen from sleeping rough to having a not too comfortable bed-sitter. He was not anxious to go back to it quickly, so he came with me to Paddington Station. As a commuter, I described some alterations they had made, indicating what it looked like before. He said: 'Gordon, you forget. I used to live here.'

One man's family just walked out on him. His son came to him in the kitchen. 'We are going now,' he said – his mother was taking him to Australia. His father hardly stirred, scarcely made a reply; he was deep in thought. He would be free now, no one to nag him, make demands on him. He would be free to gamble and live his own life. Many years later he made the effort to recover. The truth of it is that that separate world, that wonder sphere in which he lived, that magic circle round which he ran, has become an uncontrollable vortex, whirling him round and bearing him down relentlessly to the gutter, prison or even to suicide.

To whom does all this happen? Many people gamble, quite a few gamble often and heavily without getting into all this trouble. What is different about those who do? Is it all inevitable in their case? Surely, there must be a reason? Well, that is where we go next.

How does gambling take hold?

Potential problem gamblers are captivated by the rapture they find in 'action' gambling. They cannot leave it until their money is gone and even then they will try to return to it at any cost. To do so they divert money from other sources, adversely affecting themselves and their families in the process. They learn deviousness by hiding the truth of their actions from themselves. They are increasingly prepared to deceive, hurt and rob others in order to continue gambling.

Problems put them under pressure. They twist and turn to survive but will not give up their addiction. They will sacrifice anybody and anything in order to feed it. They will endure fear, loneliness, frustration, self-loathing, guilt, aggravation, degradation and loss of self-respect, all in the name of something which is destroying them.

They pursue one false hope always – to gamble their way out of their problems.

3

How does it happen?

Many readers will expect me to give a reason why some people destroy their lives in this way. Indeed, I expect that when, on page 15, I said that gambling was the root of the trouble, some of you wondered right away if we should not be looking for the root of the gambling. If you did, it was probably because we tend to believe, as I said on page 21, that gambling is a *negative* activity, exercising a negative appeal which constitutes an open invitation to deviance. The real appeal of gambling, however, is positive, and for those who respond to it, the positive attraction of 'action' gambling is so strong that it exercises a grip on their lives.

Now, it is just the nature of that grip which no member of Gamblers Anonymous has explained in my hearing. In the fellowship, it is taken for granted that everyone understands what it is. I have puzzled for years over this and recently I have found an answer which, at least for the present, satisfies me. Many others have pondered this question as well and many attempts have been made to understand and explain this kind of gambling. For that reason it has many names: 'compulsive'; 'addictive'; 'dependent'; 'pathological'; 'excessive'; and 'problem'. 'Compulsive' and 'addictive' certainly include the notion of a grip.

Gamblers Anonymous calls it 'compulsive', which is the best word for those who have been in its grip, it comes nearest to describing what goes on inside them. All the other words have something helpful to say, and each will be used as and when the context seems to make it most suitable. Mostly, however, I shall use the word 'problem' because gambling does breed problems, and it is by these problems that it can be recognized.

It may relieve some and disappoint others, but I am not going to offer any psychological or sociological explanations for problem gambling. They are there, and they are important, but I am not a psychologist or a sociologist and I did not reach my understanding of the problem with the help of those disciplines. Those who wish to follow up that aspect of the matter may be helped by the Further Reading section.

As you will have gathered from the Preface, which of course you've read, I learned all I know about problem gambling through my association with Gamblers Anonymous and Gam-Anon. On hundreds of occasions, I have listened as members have described their experiences to each other. And through listening, I believe I have come to understand.

I have learned that problem gambling can take hold of people of varied natures, temperaments and positions in life, and that it has a progressive development. Members of Gamblers Anonymous describe that progress succinctly: 'A compulsive gambler becomes a compulsive liar and a compulsive thief.' The one thing leads to the others, but how? I will try to answer that question.

We must begin by recognizing that it can happen to the best of people. The secretary of a local group of Gamblers Anonymous addressed about a hundred teenagers one Sunday evening in a Methodist Church Hall. His wife accompanied him. Prior to the meeting she said she did not wish to speak, though she was ready, if needed, to answer questions. She went to sit in the back row.

He described his life as a gambler. As soon as he had finished speaking his wife made her way to the front. There was something she had to say. Her husband must not be judged by the deeds to which he had confessed. When she married him, he was kind, considerate, reliable, helpful and loving. He had told them what he became under the influence of gambling but since he had stopped several years before, he had again become the man she married. That was the true man.

Well, how could it happen to him? How can it happen to intelligent people, whose careers require them to act responsibly? The answer is that, in each case, the person is vulnerable.

Ah! you say, now we are getting to it, but when I speak of 'vulnerability', I am not speaking of character weakness or flawed personality or anything of that kind. The vulnerability consists in the possession of four characteristics (three of which figured largely in chapter 2) which are shared by all problem gamblers. They are: The capacity to be 'taken over' by 'action' gambling; an unusually active and vivid imagination (the dream world); excessive impatience; and the capacity to become so obsessed with gambling that all of life is interpreted as a gamble. We shall deal more fully with the fourth factor later in this chapter. There is a way that it happens, rather than a reason why it happens. Members of Gamblers Anonymous recognize that they have no control over their gambling. They had to gamble, and to get the money for gambling they resorted to deception and theft which made their lives unmanageable.

That is how it came across to me, and that is how I accepted it. I saw two things, gambling, and its associated activities. Each of these presented itself to me as a circular activity, like a wheel. In the late 1960s, I wrote a brief article for *Interface*, a medical journal. I called it 'Wheel of Misfortune'. It can be summarized as follows.

'Action' gambling has a circular motion like a ferris wheel. It moves rapidly from staking to suspense (when the wheel or the card turns), from the showdown to the payment of winnings, to staking again, round and round without pause. The peak and point of the experience is not the winning but the arousal and excitement that is enjoyed as the moments of suspense follow one another rapidly. Problem gamblers are caught on that wheel in a way that others are not, and, until either all their money is gone or the 'action' ceases, they cannot stop. It is this that gives the word compulsive its special relevance, if not in the strictly medical sense.

Second, there is what I described in the article as a new merry-go-round. Whereas the first seemed to me to be vertical, this one seemed horizontal, at ground level, covering a wide area. It represented the activities associated with gambling. This circle covers miles, consumes hours, and uses up enormous amounts of energy. Movement is constant, round one circle, then round the other, back again and so on. One circle for gambling, the other to get money for gambling, two activities.

That analogy satisfied me, then one day I thought I might have spotted the difference between problem and heavy gamblers. Perhaps it is the willingness to launch into that second circle that identifies the problem gamblers – it is certainly what brings them their problems. Heavy gamblers, on the other hand, while they may forego enjoyments the rest of us would prefer, and while they may deny themselves and their families things we would consider necessary, do not ruin themselves. They may be carried along by gambling, but they are never carried away – they always know when to stop. So, is there a moment when, for the first time, the thought enters a gambler's mind that although he has run out of money he could continue to gamble if he raised the money wrongly? Is there a pause, a decision, a definite step? If that were so, and some said 'yes' while others said 'no', we would have a finger on the spot where a problem gambler might be recognized.

I put this idea to a Gamblers Anonymous friend of mine. He said at once: 'No, Gordon, it is all one thing.' All one thing – all continuous motion, no pause, no question, no decision. Perhaps members of Gamblers Anonymous were saying that a compulsive gambler *is* a compulsive liar and a compulsive thief and not changed by gambling. Yet the secretary of the group to whom I have referred was not a liar or a thief before he gambled or after he gave it up, but it all belongs together in some way.

I was thrown back on my heels. I thought again and remembered an experience from 1963, the year before Gamblers Anonymous came to London. Charles Kenna, an Australian, a lecturer in psychology at the University of New South Wales, in Sydney, was here on a year's sabbatical leave, investigating addiction to gambling, which he had met over there. I had met Charles several times so I knew what to say when, one day, I had a call from Michael Sorenson. He was then a welfare officer at Pentonville Prison. He had gathered a group of men whose crimes, so he discovered, were related directly to their gambling. Did I know anyone who could go over there and help them?

I took Charles Kenna and soon we were sitting round a table with Michael and about twelve inmates. The conversation was lively. Suddenly Charles asked, 'What other experience comes nearest to gambling?' With one voice and great conviction, they said: 'Being on the job.'

It was clear what they meant. You have seen the point already. To plot and carry through a confidence trick or to break and enter premises in order to steal, involves taking a risk. You stake your freedom in the hope of getting away with a prize. It is akin to gambling. What I did not realize at the time, nor for a long while afterwards, was how much like gambling all that is. When this experience came back to me I knew that these men were not making any academic comparisons between two forms of risk taking. They were saying that 'being on the job' was 'action', just as gambling was 'action' and that both produced the same intensified and elevated state of mind, the same arousal, the same buzz.

So, suddenly, I saw that it is indeed one thing, a continuity of gambling. *A problem gambler is one who is so obsessed with gambling that he interprets life in that way. He gambles at the tables, at the races, on the machines and he also gambles when he sets out to get the money for what we call gambling in the ordinary sense of the word.* When he does that, he stakes everything: his home, his family, his job, his serenity, his self-respect and his life. Problems, serious problems, are part and parcel of problem gambling. The expression 'compulsive gambling' is especially relevant here in understanding the gambler's experience of being driven round and round these two circles.

Having reached that point, I remembered a member of a prison group of Gamblers Anonymous. Perhaps he was in his early thirties. He recounted the story of his last days of freedom just prior to this sentence, one of several. He had had to leave home again because of the problems created by his gambling and for a few weeks he engaged in gambling and petty crime, sleeping rough. He was going nowhere, but the way he was driven through it all gave it a fearful purpose. As I listened, I felt tired, worn out, in sympathy. At last he spoke of the policeman's hand on his shoulder. It was a relief, such a relief, he said, to stop: to stop the whole thing, the one continuous and inclusive activity of gambling.

Perhaps that is why, if a recovered gambler returns to gambling, he returns to the whole experience. People do not, as a rule, the second time around, play themselves into gambling and then develop the problems. The obsession is there, full grown, at once. Several who have returned to Gamblers Anonymous after falling back into gambling, have made that point. 'I was straight back there,' said one. 'All the old thinking returned at once.' That must be a horrifying experience. Indeed, in one year, four men in young middle life took their own lives when they gambled again after some years of abstinence. I knew them all, one of them well. His contribution to Gamblers Anonymous, locally and nationally, was great and as a Toast Master, his voluntary services at our daughter's wedding made all the difference to the day. He gave much to many people but problem gambling broke him.

The next question to ask is, When and how does a problem gambler break free from his obsession?

Gambling's grip can make good people bad

The most vulnerable are those who:

- can be 'taken over' by gambling,
- have an exceptionally vivid imagination (dream world),
- and have excessive impatience.

Even for these there is always a way to be followed. If they meet 'action' gambling they will be captivated by it. Next they will find that they need it enough to lie and steal to return to it. Lying and stealing will give them the same excitement that they find in gambling, and eventually they will become so obsessed with gambling that they will interpret the whole of life as a gamble and live it that way, putting all at risk.

This condition is known as *compulsive, addictive, dependent, pathological, excessive* or *problem* gambling, but *problem* gambling is probably the best name, as it breeds problems and can be identified by the nature of them.

4

Where does it stop?

Gamblers Anonymous states that compulsive gamblers seek help when they reach 'rock bottom'. They suffer an acute crisis – personal rather than financial – which shocks them out of their obsession and forces them to face the truth about themselves. One day in the late 1960s, a man came into my office in the early evening in such a condition. He put a bottle of tablets on my desk. Was there any reason, he asked, why he should not take the lot? He had been discharged from prison a year earlier, having served a sentence for embezzlement. He came out determined to go straight: one marriage had ended through gambling, and his career had been badly affected. He knew that his common-law wife, having taken him back on his release, would not tolerate any more gambling, so he had hung on and not gambled, until, that is, a short time before.

He had secured employment as a deputy accountant, and his employer knew nothing of his previous sentence. He had done well so far and, because the accountant was soon to retire, he was expecting to be promoted. Then, one day at lunch, he met a man he had known in prison. They talked for a while and before they parted his friend gave him a tip for a race that afternoon, a *certainty*. The nature of this conversation is important. The friend would be someone like himself, in the con-man class, perhaps another gambler. Each would wish to convince the other of his present success. The dream world imaginings would get to work, and the pictures they painted would get larger and brighter. So a fertile soil was prepared into which the tip for the race fell like a seed. His excited frame of mind stirred up the impatience and there he was, opening his office safe, taking a hundred pounds from the cash which he controlled, and hurrying to a bookmaker's to get the bet on. The bet lost, but the 'action' dream world and impatience (the last perhaps experienced largely as fear), got to him none the less. In a short space of time, he had stolen a considerable amount of money from his firm and was about to face the consequences because the auditors were expected in a few days.

I do not know if he was serious about committing suicide. He may have hoped that the threat of it would blackmail someone into giving him the money to put things right. I put away the tablets and told him I thought he would go to prison and lose his wife if things were as he described them. There was still the future, though. He agreed to go with me that night to Gamblers Anonymous. The meeting gave him the resolution to face everything, come what may. The wife of another member went to speak to his wife who agreed to stay with him, provided he gave up gambling. A fellow member went with him to see his employer who, when it was agreed that the money should be repaid, kept him on and eventually promoted him.

The story does not always have such a fairy-tale ending. Another man, who attended the first meeting of Gamblers Anonymous in London, was in a similar situation. He was a milkman and had been defrauding his company, gambling the proceeds and falsifying his accounts. He was to see the manager the following morning. Henry, the American who brought Gamblers Anonymous to the UK (and whom we met in the Preface), went with him to meet his employer, and to the court when he was tried. He received a year's probation. He lost his job, but found a new one in which he did not handle money, and eventually he paid back what he owed. He stayed with Gamblers Anonymous.

Going to Gamblers Anonymous does not necessarily mean that a prison sentence can be avoided. One afternoon a man burst into my office. He was desperate – he was employed by a chain of television retailers delivering sets and receiving payments, frequently in cash. He had systematically embezzled money from these payments for gambling. He had been discovered and was afraid that, because of his previous convictions, the court would deal with him very seriously this time.

I persuaded him to go with me to the shop where he was based. Perhaps he hoped I would persuade his employers not to charge him. If so, it was a vain hope, he had to be charged under a company rule. They telephoned the police. He tensed, ready to rise saying, 'Now you are going to make me run.' Somehow, by word and gesture, I restrained him. Probably he knew how futile running would be and was glad to be restrained. He was taken to the police station, charged, taken before the magistrate and remanded on bail for trial. That night and once or twice immediately afterwards he went to Gamblers Anonymous and opened his mind to what he heard, and acted upon it. When, just short of a year later, he was released from prison, he came straight to see me, radiant and free from gambling. He had clearly benefited from his prison sentence. The previous ones had made him worse, but this time it was different because he faced it properly, he knew he had deserved it. He was not filled with resentment. He made living through it a part of his recovery.

The events which lead problem gamblers to seek help are not always so dramatic. Let me tell you of two men who, when I met them, had been married for many years and had gambled for at least as many. In both cases their wives and children had had enough, and both of them were ready for a personal crisis.

The younger of the two had recently 'celebrated' his silver wedding. There had been no money for celebration and no real marriage to celebrate. Now it was his wife's birthday and again there was no money and no present. She did not look for one – she would not miss what she did not expect. The impact of his failure fell on him. All the failures down the years had reduced him to a weariness of self-contempt and self-loathing. He read about Gamblers Anonymous in the press and went to the first meeting in London. He was sick and tired of gambling and said so. He accepted the challenge to stop gambling and at once proceeded with his recovery. The next week his wife accompanied him and attended Gam-Anon.

The other was equally ready for his personal crisis. One evening, returning home, he found his wife prepared to leave him, her bag packed at the door, their married daughter waiting to take her home with her. He capitulated, welcomed the ultimatum. He would accept help. They went together that night to Gamblers Anonymous and Gam-Anon. They found what they needed and never looked back.

Not every gambler takes so long to reach rock bottom. For one man, one small crime was enough. A friend of his wanted a medallion of which a limited issue had been struck for a national commemoration. He could not obtain one, but our gambler could. Just give him £70 and he would get it.

It was foolish, like most things problem gamblers do to raise funds. He had to be found out, the friend would be round for the medal. When he was confronted the shame was too great. He came to Gamblers Anonymous and stayed for many months to make sure he was back in his right mind. He and his family were lucky it happened so quickly.

The personal crisis of which we have been speaking, as opposed to a financial crisis, is called the 'rock bottom experience'. We must think about it for a while to understand what it is. It is well known that rock bottom for one is three-quarters or half-way down for another. Apart from suicide, there seems to be no absolute bottom, no place where you absolutely must stop, no point where the only way is upwards. There are, however, ledges on the way down. Previously, we have called them crises. Hit one of those and you are temporarily halted, you suffer shock, pain, alarm, desperation. If you make no sense of it but turn and run, or try to scheme your way out of it, you are off the ledge and falling again. Any ledge, though, can provide a rock bottom experience, provided that, as well as feeling the pain, you see that there is a way up. Indeed, you must see that up is the way and that you must take it.

Most gamblers need help at that point. They need someone to turn their head upwards. Usually it is a member of the family, but for one man it was his bookmaker who was also his friend. When the bookmaker realized what was happening to his friend he refused him further credit. When other bookmakers gave it and his friend saw that he was endangering his family and his professional standing, he found out about Gamblers Anonymous and encouraged his friend's wife to face her husband. Helped in that way, she found new hope and courage and between them they landed him in Gamblers Anonymous. There, within two weeks, though unwilling at first, he found he *had* reached rock bottom. He would have missed it but for that intervention. Afterwards, he described this somewhat differently. He said he had been falling down and down when, suddenly, a parachute opened and saved him from the gutter. His friend, his wife, the members of Gamblers Anonymous and Gam-Anon, had put their hands under him and he settled gently on his rock bottom ledge.

Intervention can come from many quarters and could come much earlier and more often from the helping agencies which frequently deal with problem gamblers and their families, though they may not know it. Such families seek help for many reasons. They tend to hide their secret, and present only financial difficulties, debt, family tension, bad 'nerves' or inability to sleep. Sometimes, when they do speak up, a doctor, or probation officer or a social worker will recommend them to Gamblers Anonymous and Gam-Anon. In too many cases, however, those who serve the helping agencies lack sufficient information about problem gambling and so fail to recognize it when they meet it. (This theme is taken up again in chapter 9). Do not think that you can intervene successfully whenever you choose. The time must be ripe. In the meantime, while any feeling remains, while there is any desire for reconciliation and for the restoration of a proper family life, partners and families hang on. The waiting time does not have to be passive, however. You must try to expedite that personal crisis, but what you do in that direction can and should have a positive and immediate purpose. That purpose is to defend yourself against the effects of the gambling and protect your own inward life instead of just letting it be eroded away. This is the subject of the next chapter.

Where does the gambling stop?

You cannot talk a gambler into stopping. You cannot trap a gambler into stopping.

You cannot force a gambler to stop. He needs first to reach his 'rock bottom'.

A 'rock bottom' is a frightening personal crisis that temporarily stops his fall and leads him to look around for help. It is not an absolute bottom but a ledge. You can help him while he is on that ledge. Friends can help him. Colleagues can help him. The caring professions can help him. Above all, the family can help him.

Nagging, badgering, bullying, will not help, but if you try to show him that there is a way back up again and that he can take it and that you will give him all the support he wants while he is trying, you may succeed.

5

Cry, 'Hold, enough'

We have returned to the wife (or husband or parent) we left at the end of chapter 1, turned in upon herself, lost, with her mind going round in circles. She may find it impossible to believe, but the initiative for change lies with her. She may laugh bitterly when she reads that. Well, let me talk to her. I know you cannot change your gambler, you cannot even control your efforts to do so. By the time things have reached an advanced stage, you will have become so frustrated by the pathetic excuses, lies, deceptions, betrayals, and broken promises that even if you do try to reason with him you will be overcome by a desire to punish him, to make him suffer. Bitterness, contempt, resentment and hatred master you, and all your attempts end in screaming failure. Then your passion dies, your resolve collapses, and you sink once again in shame into your usual condition of humiliating helplessness. You are beaten and you know it.

On his side, he has learned to take advantage of this. See it from his point of view. A man of about 30 years of age sat with his mother, his sister and his wife. One after the other they went for him, venting their feelings. He sat it out, saying nothing. He had been through all this before. He knew that when they had worn themselves out one of them would give him some money with which he would go to the greyhounds that evening.

That old way of doing things must stop. You must take a new direction, change the rhythm, alter the pattern. You cannot change *him*. It is you, yourself, who must change. For this, you need help and help of the right kind and in the best way is available. At the end of the telephone someone is waiting to listen to you. She (it probably will be she) will once have endured the tension you are now suffering and will have screwed up the courage to make the call you now want to make.

You can depend on anonymity. In fact you can make sure of it. If your name is Jane, you can call yourself Mary. No one will mind and when, later, you explain, everyone will understand why you did it. You will not be asked for your full name or your address. You do not even have to give anyone your telephone number – though you may wish to do so after just one conversation.

You will probably have heard of Gamblers Anonymous or, if you are the parent of a child gambler, you may have noticed something in the Press, on radio or television, about Parents of Young Gamblers. Gamblers Anonymous is for compulsive (or problem) gamblers who have accepted that they have no control over gambling and who are helping themselves and each other to stop gambling and to make their lives manageable again. Gam-Anon is for relatives and friends (usually wives) of compulsive gamblers who are helping themselves and each other restore their lives. Parents of Young Gamblers is much younger and is for parents of child gamblers who do not admit that they have a problem and will not accept help. It puts parents in touch with each other for mutual support, encouragement and advice.

All three have literature to send you. Telephone directories give a number for Gamblers Anonymous, and that is the number to use for Gam-Anon if it is not listed separately. If your directory has no number, in the UK you can try your local Citizens' Advice Bureau or the Samaritans: they can often put you in touch with a group or a member. Otherwise you can ring 01 352 3060, 021 233 1335, 061 273 3574, 0742 25596 (daytime), 041 445 1115 or for Eire 300 993, whichever is nearest to you. There may not be a group right on your doorstep, but you will be put in touch with someone not too far away. The British number for Parents of Young Gamblers is 021 633 4771. When you phone you will be put in touch with the nearest member. There are many, but if none is near you or if you are outside the UK, you should try Gam-Anon. Anyone with a gambling problem, their own or that of another, is welcome to contact any of these fellowships at any time. Members are only too ready to share the help they themselves have received.

A word of warning. Neither Gamblers Anonymous, Gam-Anon, nor Parents of Young Gamblers, has a fully staffed office, funds do not run to it. You may therefore come across an answering machine or be advised by an operator to ring an alternative number on which a member is receiving calls. Please do not be put off by that. Be brave and determined – you are telephoning to save your life.

After a few calls, probably after the first, you will trust the voice at the other end of the telephone. When you do trust, even just one voice, and pour out your story, one significant knot of the tangle of your inner person and your life will have been unravelled. If at all possible, go to a meeting as well. On the telephone, or at the meeting, you will learn what you can do about your own situation. Just getting things off your chest helps straighten things out. To give you an idea of what else can happen, I will tell you about one gambler's wife who telephoned for help.

The son of a well-to-do professional man who had been given a good start in life had slipped down and down through gambling. When I met him he was employed changing coins in an amusement arcade in Soho. He lived with his wife and baby son in a flat above a shop in an unfashionable street in one of London's older and greyer suburbs.

His wife had a good job, and found herself not only maintaining the home but also giving him money for his weekly needs and paying his debts. She telephoned for help and spoke to me and to a member of Gam-Anon. Her husband was not prepared to go to Gamblers Anonymous or to stop gambling. Soon she began to look on things objectively and it was suggested that she should make a stand on one issue – she settled upon the matter of money for the house. She faced him and said that, in future, she would expect a certain sum from him each week. Taken by surprise, he agreed and, for a few weeks, abided by this agreement. It was not long, however, before she made an urgent call to Gam-Anon one afternoon from her office. Her husband had just telephoned with an excuse for not having the whole amount that week. She played for time, saying she was busy and would ring him back. She asked what should she say to him. It was pointed out to her that if she agreed to a lower sum this week the same thing was likely to happen again.

She was firm when she returned his call and he found all the money that week and for a few more weeks. Then he began to bring smaller amounts with a different excuse each time. Again she telephoned, and this time it was suggested that she might give him a choice, either to bear his proper share of the household expenses or stop living there. It was important that she should think out well how to say this. She should make it clear that she loved him – that is why she married him. For the same reason she wanted to carry on living with him, but she could not do that while he continued to gamble. It was not just the gambling. The lies, deceit and uncertainty that it entailed were poisoning their relationship. If he was going to continue gambling he would have to leave. She wanted him to stop gambling and stay, the choice was his.

He went. He packed his bag and moved out. Now she really need-ed support, she was on the telephone every few days. Had she done the right thing? Would he be all right? Would he be hungry or sleep-ing rough? Might he have gone abroad, committed suicide? She was assured that he would be all right and probably come home soon.

He came back after two weeks. He had found a room in the next street but he had been miserable. He had secretly watched her as she went to work and as she came home in the evening. He settled down for a while to make regular payments to the housekeeping and, although he gambled periodically, they managed much better for the next year or so. We shall return to them at the end of this chapter.

Let us assume, then, that you want the gambling to end, to have the true person back again, and that you are willing to hold out and work for that. Chapters 2, 3 and 4 will have helped you. From them, you will know that your gambler is in the grip of what is virtually an illness and that, although everything he does seems deliberate, a great deal is beyond his control. While he gambles, you still feel resentment but, if any feeling towards him remains, try to maintain as much of a human relationship with him as is possible. I hardly dare use the words love and caring, though what they stand for may persist, even if in shreds.

If you keep open the lifeline to Gam-Anon (or, if you are a parent, to Parents of Young Gamblers) you will be able to hold to your pur-pose. They will not get tired of you if you are really trying. It will be understood that you may fail from time to time, falling back into your old helplessness or bitter frenzies. While he continues to gam-ble you will be subjected to the same buffeting for money, buffeting of lies and buffeting of crises, but with the help of Gam-Anon or Parents of Young Gamblers you will be able to withstand it. After all you are standing up for your life – and his. If you can get to some meetings you will be amazed and grateful for the relief and strength you find there.

You will also gain a clearer head and a new confidence. That con-fidence can be enhanced by some financial independence. You may have a job or perhaps you can get one, possibly part time. Whether or not you can do that you have to find ways of recovering and defending your personal independence. You have become more and more like a puppet on his string. Take time and think. There are bound to be many things on which you want to make a stand, but choose *one* on which you think you can do so successfully. It may be small, but it must matter. Do not bluff and do not threaten what you cannot carry out. Don't let yourself deviously think, 'This will bring him to his senses.' You are trying simply to find your feet again and stand on them.

Whatever you do it will seem to him that you are acting against him, being awkward, uncooperative and unreasonable. He may respond violently – you will have surprised and frightened him. He has come to depend on being able to manipulate you. He will feel uncertain, apprehensive. He will probably bluff, bully, cajole, plead and threaten by turns. He will use emotional blackmail and subject you to every kind of pressure of which he is capable to make you once again amenable to his wishes. You will have to look to your defences now because, when you make your stand, you will, from time to time, question your own motives. Your old antagonistic attitude towards him will remain and what he says and does will revive that, as well as the guilt and shame you have always felt in consequence. That is likely to weaken you. Try not to let that happen. Remember that in seeking your own recovery you are doing the best you can to seek his too. Above all, any nagging must cease – you cannot change him – and you must cease settling his financial problems for him – if you continue to do this it will only encourage him to go on gambling. We learned earlier that he gets to his rock bottom when the responsibility for gambling and the debts and other problems it brings press hard on him. Pain wakes you out of sleep, fear rouses you from a nightmare. A crisis can bring a gambler face to face with the reality of his situation. The more you look after your interests and those of the family, the more you help him reach that experience.

You *do* have allies – they are the friends who have deserted him, employers who parted company with him, banks, building societies and loan companies who press for repayment, and creditors who take out court orders against him. All these compel him to race more rapidly, more desperately, round wider and wider circles, trying somehow to get out of trouble.

In the end, he has only you and perhaps your family and his family. His next crisis is your opportunity. There is no guarantee that it will work but, if you have made your stand, he may hear you say that there is now no more running, nowhere to go, that the time has come to stop and face up to things. You know where to find help and, if he will take it, he can count on your support. You will help with this, but you will no longer help him out in the old way. He must choose. Because he is likely to retain his old exterior to the last, you may hesitate to challenge him, but remember that the exterior is misleading. Underneath it is a different story – he is eaten away by guilt and undermined by loss of self-respect. He will be glad of your strength. He needs to change, and, through all his confusion, he knows it. Get him on the 'phone to a member of Gamblers Anonymous right away. Make sure, though, that you and he quickly get to a meeting. If you do not, you and your family may drift back where you came from. This happened to the husband and wife we were talking about earlier. Neither attended Gamblers Anonymous or Gam-Anon even once. Had they done so they might have made a real recovery. But as it was, from my fairly close association with them over a few years, I know that he gambled again, frequently making trouble for himself. She was never overwhelmed by it, though. She learned how to live with it and with him and to make gambling and its results his problem, until, that is, the last time I heard from them.

She telephoned to say that he was now in debt to a very dangerous person who was looking for him and likely to do him real harm. She asked me to act as a go-between and ask a relative of his to help them out. I did as I was asked but I heard no more. I do not know what happened to them but I know that if you do not get right out of trouble you may fall right back in again, deeper than ever. Of course, your gambling partner may refuse to go to Gamblers Anonymous. If he does, you should go to Gam-Anon just the same. He may do all he can to prevent you, but you will need the support Gam-Anon can give you more than ever and you will be most welcome. You will grow stronger, and you will see things from a better perspective. You will increase your understanding of gambling, and of him and your bitterness will decrease. You will recover your proper self. You may learn to talk with him about things other than gambling. You will be able to accept him for what he is and at the same time decide whether or not you want to stay with him. All that is far from perfect, but take what you have. You have no control over his gambling but *your* life need not be unmanageable.

Imagine now a long pause on my part. I have thought about the contents of this chapter, and I am now thinking about its impact on a gambler's wife as she reads it. Perhaps I have made it all seem too easy, giving the impression that she can so quickly get into a calm frame of mind. My difficulty is that I have learned about these things from Gam-Anon, in the company of people who, in that fellowship, have achieved a remarkable serenity. No doubt the experiences of which they spoke were vastly more stressful than the language or tone of voice they used in describing them. I will try to put the balance right by telling you how one woman described the way she and her husband came to Gamblers Anonymous and to Gam-Anon.

After many years of gambling and deception, he telephoned home one evening to say he was visiting a friend, but in the background she heard the whirr of a roulette wheel. It was the last straw. She was furious. When he came home there was a row and she demanded over and over again how much he had lost. Obviously he did not tell her but their relationship reached a crisis and he went with her to Gamblers Anonymous. It lasted three weeks, he did not need them, he said, he could stop on his own. A few months later things got so bad that she knew they must go again. She could not cope any more with life and if he was only half an hour late getting home, her stomach was in knots. She took him to Gamblers Anonymous and 12 months later they were still succeeding. The real thing will look much more like this struggle but, don't forget, the initiative for going to the meetings was *hers*. *She* had been in touch with Gam-Anon, and *she* did not forget.

You can take the initiative for change

- Change yourself, not the gambler.
- Clear your head and concentrate on regaining your confidence.
- Stop behaving like a puppet on a string and find your own independent person.

You will need help. Get in touch with Gam-Anon. Keep in touch with them. They will help you to understand your situation. With their guidance and support, you will be able to take a new direction, and make a stand – change the old destructive pattern.

Allow the gambler to take responsibility for his addiction and the problems it is causing. This will surprise and frighten him at first and may arouse his resentment and hostility, but ultimately it will help him to find his 'rock bottom'. Always make it clear that you are on his side, and watch for the moment to get close to him to give him support. Then (at the next crisis) he will know that there is help and an answer.

Get him to Gamblers Anonymous as soon as possible.

6
How does Gamblers Anonymous work?

Members of Gamblers Anonymous frequently ask each other, 'How does Gamblers Anonymous work?' This is a largely rhetorical question. Over the first weeks, perhaps after the first night, stress and tension have diminished. They are not gambling. They have wakened from a nightmare into a new day, acting, thinking and living differently. They are refreshed and rejuvenated, new people in a new world. They even look different. Overweight people become slimmer, and overthin people put on weight. Their eyes clear and their expressions change. I remember failing to recognize one man. When he spoke, his story became familiar. I had seen him as a first night member four weeks earlier. When I realized who he was, I saw how much his facial and general appearance had changed.

The first changes in personality, too, can take place very quickly. How can this be, when they felt themselves powerless to change before? Surely, it would have required surgery, drugs, hypnosis or at least electric shocks to the brain to bring about such a change so fast! In fact, all there was was some meetings, people, a few pamphlets, a simple programme of actions they had been recommended to take, and the miracle had happened. How? Any effect requires an efficient cause. In this case, what was the cause?

It is possible that the secret lies in an understanding of three expressions, repeated over and over again by successive 'generations' of members of Gamblers Anonymous. They are: 'When I came through that door'; 'in the room'; and 'in GA'. These words are spoken intensely, seriously, indeed, in awe. I believe they epitomize crucial experiences through which the speaker and his hearers have passed, and are still passing.

The references to 'the door' and 'the room' have a strong physical and topographical reference but they are used metaphorically. Members still refer to 'that door' and 'this room', even when they have travelled a long way to visit each others' meetings. Similarly, the expression 'in GA' means much more than just membership of the fellowship. 'Coming through the door' speaks of impact, of a totally new experience. I can find no words to explain it more fully but as you read on you will discover what I think the expression signifies. The significance of the 'room' also lies in what is experienced there. In that room, lives are changed and each week strength to live a new life is restored.

Being 'in GA' is a state of life. It is an experience that goes with members wherever they go. It would be as true to say that GA is in them. How could they succeed unless what they saw when they went in through that 'door' and experienced in that 'room' went out with them? Between meetings, they are on their own, picking their way through an environment which is, for them, full of danger, trying to put into practice ideas to which, perhaps even just the week before, they were strangers. There is more to recovery than just staying away from gambling, as will appear in a later chapter.

The 'room', the 'door', and 'being in GA' enable Gamblers Anonymous to work because they provide an antidote to the gambling experience. It, too, had its 'door'. When they first experience it, 'action' gambling makes a tremendous impact on all problem or compulsive gamblers. There is also a 'room': the casino, the betting office, the racecourse or the track, the bingo hall, the venue for the gaming machines. Further, those who become addicted are 'in gambling', and gambling is in them, day after day, night after night, week after week and year after year, until the spell is broken. That spell can be broken in Gamblers Anonymous because it answers door for door, room for room and spell for spell. Of course, the desire for gambling disappears quickly only for some. They are the ones who are truly sick and tired of it. Some who find they are not yet ready to give it up will probably not return for a second meeting. For many, resisting the call of the 'action' is a struggle which continues for years. If giving up gambling was all that there is to it, I can imagine that it would be a boring, dreary and depressing business.

In Gamblers Anonymous, however, there truly is a spell. This is the experience of being 'in GA'. Members who feel the need to do so, return to the 'room' at least once and often twice or more a week to reinforce the experience. If they follow the programme, that spell, as we shall see, is also cast over their lives. Very soon that new life means so much that it would be harder to give up than gambling, however hard that might be. So there is a 'spell' and plenty of 'magic' as well. There is no magic cure, however. Indeed, because there is no absolute reason, no cause for the gambling, there is no cure. Rather, there is a way to recover from problem gambling, just as there was a way into it. The 'spell' does not hold everyone who comes, as we said above. We shall think again of those who either do not return or only come back a few times in chapter 9.

The first essential is re-orientation, to 'come through the door', to find 'the room'. It is amazing how naturally this is done. Perhaps, because there has been a previous telephone call, someone is there early, on the lookout for the new member; just as likely, he will be seen hovering about the door or outside the building. Because everyone comes in the same state of mind, the signs can be read and an approach made. Contact is made quietly. First names are exchanged and you will be introduced to other members if it happens naturally. There is no fuss. New members are not overwhelmed, but from the first handshake they are aware of being both welcomed and understood. That combination comes as a shock to the problem gambler, it is the first 'impact', the beginning of the experience of the 'door'. Problem gamblers are accustomed to being shunned by those they know; with strangers, they put on an elaborate 'front' to hide what they really are. Now they are not only accepted, but made welcome, and welcomed not just as they are, but *because* of what they are. Nothing has been said, but everything seems to be known. And despite this, they are treated as acceptable people. That is something to think about.

There is something special, too, about the people who greet them. They have an air of authority, they take charge, but quietly. They are confident, but not arrogant. They lead the way into that room as if it contained the whole answer to the whole of life. They are not saints, but they know that they know the answers. There is no badgering. Someone will listen if you want to say something. People will smile, nod, and say a few words of greeting but no one will ask you anything but your first name. You will be invited to sit down and, clearly, sitting is relaxing and resting to the extent that your inward mental and spiritual turmoil will allow. Other members arrive, the Chairman and Secretary take their places, and the meeting begins. You will be welcomed. The Chairman may have been told you are there or he may enquire if there are any new members. You may be asked to stand up and give your first name. As you sit down you will be clapped heartily. How's that for impact? When did that last happen to you? What have you now done to deserve it?

Probably then, at the Chairman's direction, people will begin to read from a pamphlet, either whole passages or sentence by sentence round the room. You will have a copy and, as far as you can, you follow the words, but it is doubtful if you will grasp much of the meaning. You may be asked to read a sentence, and it will be a wonder if you do not stumble over it. You are beginning to experience the 'room'.

Something is going on, there is no doubt about that, something good, something important, yet something which can be expressed in simple words. It is about gambling – or about not gambling, which you suppose you expected. Then it dawns on you that something may happen to *you*.

The 12 steps of the Recovery Programme will be read. (You can see it on page 122). It is written in the past tense, which is good. The steps are presented as accomplishments, as if achieved by those already here and by others in years gone by. They give the impression that this is a success room, and that where others have gone new members can follow. You do not feel you have to understand them right away as you would if they were expressed as commands which must be obeyed at once. As months go by, the words may work their way into your mind and you will discover that you have shared the experience they describe.

The meeting and what happens there must constitute a surprise. What did you expect? A man seated at a table with a fistful of money, asking how much you needed to get out of trouble? A sort of vicar's tea-party? A few do-gooders asking you questions, working you over, getting you to fill out a questionnaire? A pathetic group of down-and-outs presided over by a social worker or a psychiatrist? One thing is certain, you will not have expected what you found, even if, correctly, you were told that Gamblers Anonymous is for compulsive gamblers. You could never have imagined this gathering of ordinary, respectable people. They say they used to hang out in betting offices and all those other places where you gambled. Why don't they look as though they did? After the readings, the Chairman will invite each member in turn to give his 'therapy'. As he does so he will remind everyone that anything spoken in the room is in confidence, and that *nothing* may be repeated outside. Each tells his own story, his gambling experiences and what has happened to him since he came to Gamblers Anonymous. He will begin by identifying himself, giving his first name and adding, 'and I am a compulsive gambler'. He will probably also say how long it is since he has gambled. It is likely each one will address part of what he says directly to you. He may tell you that, as a new member, you are the most

important person in that room. You will probably not be very recep-
tive. Your body may be still, but your nerves are jumping and your
mind is in a whirl. For moments at a time, though, you can concentrate and hear what is being said. You may say to yourself, 'That person is describing my life.' Even after that, there may not be too many
clear, consecutive thoughts. There will be impressions, though, and
these, if you are going to succeed, will later come to the surface of
your mind. At least, you will appreciate that these are compulsive
gamblers and that you understand them and what they are saying.
From that, sooner or later, you will realize how it was that they
understood you, and why, when you entered the room, they did not
need to interrogate you. You will also gather that every person there
arrived in the room in deep trouble just as you have done and that
they are working their way out of it.

Some things that are said are painful even to hear. Men are
haunted by the way in which they have persistently and deliberately
taken advantage of their mothers and grandmothers, wasting their
savings, even their weekly pensions, preying mercilessly on the very
people with the weakest defences against their pressure, cunning and
deceit. One man told of how his gambling led him to kill a child.
Because of his gambling he neglected his car, and the tyres were bald.
One wet day, desperate to get a bet on in a certain race, he hurried
from his place of employment, jumped into his car, and drove far
too quickly for safety. As he went over a bridge, his car skidded on
the wet surface and crushed a child of eight against a wall. Such
things are agonizing to hear, and worse to recall and confess, but
they must come out.

Another spoke of what he had done to his wife. For years his
gambling had inflicted on her mental suffering and physical want.
Now, in her plight, she humiliated herself, following him into the
lobby of a London gaming club (casino). She pleaded with him to
come home, not to gamble, not to lose more money. They were in
desperate trouble. The money he had at that moment had been
raised by an additional mortgage on their house to pay pressing
debts. Yet he rejected her, callously, violently, and went into the
club to gamble. He knew she could not follow him because she was
not a member of the club and he would not make her his guest.
Moreover, the management would not permit a disturbance. He
looked back on what he had done, horrified, almost with unbelief.
In a voice taut with pain, he said, 'I just left her there – in all her
misery – I just left her there.'

It is not all so intense. I remember the tone of voice in which a young man said he had no right to take all those liberties with all those people. He spoke quietly, judging and rejecting yesterday's self. He saw for what they were the dirty little tricks by which he had inconvenienced, often seriously, the people concerned. He had used them as a means to his ends.

Another young man, arriving at Gamblers Anonymous shortly after being released from prison, spoke quietly of the way he was facing and apologizing to the people against whom he had offended. 'It was not easy for me', he said, 'to tell that man that I had stolen from his shop and the other that I had taken his bicycle.' Another member told how he sometimes entertained friends at home to concerts of recorded music. As the guests departed he was at the door, not just to say goodbye, but also to touch them for any money they had in their pockets.

It may have appeared, when I said that people would address part of their therapy directly to new members, that the purpose of making these statements and admissions is to help each other. They do have that effect, but it is a by-product. Each member speaks from his own need to do so. Fundamentally, each one is there for himself. Each needs to stop gambling, to stay stopped and to recover his life. He benefits from hearing the others but he needs to make his own statement. Only by revealing himself to others can he be sure he has faced himself.

We often speak of the need to get things off our chests, but the gambler's need goes much deeper than that. Another metaphor is needed. Having attended meetings for about twelve weeks, one first-night member in London said to me, 'Gordon, I don't have the same need now to give a therapy. It has been like taking daggers out of wounds so that the wounds could heal.'

Confessions are received with a quiet seriousness. Sometimes, however, the room is filled with laughter. Problem gamblers, in thrall to their dream world, often make fools of themselves. 'How could I have been such a fool', a man will say, and describe how he conceived and tried to carry through a complicated scheme which would get him out of trouble and win him a fortune, only to be humiliated when it all fell flat.

The 'room' is the place where all this can be done. Elsewhere, such statements would be received with dismay and disgust and flung back in the speaker's face. *But in the meetings of Gamblers Anonymous, attitudes are wonderfully balanced. The secret is that nothing is condemned and nothing is condoned.* It is understood that, given the circumstances, people can do the terrible things gamblers talk about. It is understood that if, having done them, a person turns from them, that person must be accepted as if he had not done them. It is also understood that, to lead a normal life among normal people, that person must never do any such thing again. Whatever is spoken is accepted and placed on the table and then discarded. The speaker, having faced what he has done, is now free to make amends. (We shall discuss this in later chapters.)

Identification with others, bringing, as it does, understanding of oneself, is the high point of the experience of being 'in the room'. There has always been self-knowledge, of a kind, but until now, the gambler has always run away to hide from it. Now, having faced and recognized himself in other people, he can gratefully accept the common label: he is a 'compulsive gambler'. It is a relief; if he were not, he would be either mad or bad. He accepts that being a compulsive gambler is a kind of sickness, and in accepting that, he can accept himself. He does not need to run any more, he can stop, stop gambling, stop all that feverish activity and find out what comes next.

This brings him to the moment when he can complete the process of experiencing the 'room'. He is ready to give his own therapy. This may or may not be on the first night and, in any case, it will not be easy. The recollections which crowd in on him will probably be fairly disorganized. Where should he start? He speaks as much to himself as to the people around him, if not more so. So far as he is concerned, this therapy is happening to him alone. Even when he settles upon an event which must be shared, the sequence in which things occurred may not be clear to him. He may have to correct himself many times. Not only has he been running away from all this for a long time but he is now looking at everything from a new point of view.

There are exceptions. As more and more people came to the meetings, I noticed that some would give a therapy at their first meeting, easily, without hesitation, and in logical order. They gave the impression of 'having got the message' straightaway. I would look for them the following week. Often, to my surprise, they would not be there. As time went on I began to recognize a pattern, though not a rule. It dawned on me that it was possible that these people never really entered at all into the situation but merely sized it up and decided to conform to it for that evening to avoid embarrassment. It was not what they wanted, at least not at that time. On the other hand it was quite remarkable how often people came back whom most members expected not to see again. They had been too confused to have any experience of the 'door' or the 'room'. Those experiences and that of being 'in GA' do not come in a sequence, the second following the first and the third following the second, they are aspects of each other, parts of one whole experience. Indeed, being 'in GA' may be the first feeling to make its presence felt. One man, when the meeting was over, accepted a lift to the nearest underground station and was given the fare for his journey home. He waved goodbye, turning as if to go into the station. When the car was out of sight he set off to walk, thinking of a club where he could get a game that night and where he hoped his little windfall could be turned into a stake for a proper gamble. On his way, his mind turned over what he had heard. People there had experienced life, not beyond the grave, but beyond the sack, beyond eviction and beyond a prison sentence. Their self-respect had been restored. Perhaps he could find life beyond the general rottenness into which he had sunk. He walked on home and returned the following week, a new look in his eyes and a new expectation in his heart. He was already 'in GA' and GA was in him. Because of that, in recollection, he had passed through 'the door' and into 'the room'.

In this chapter we have dealt with re-orientation which is stage one of the recovery programme. It is rather like re-setting a compass. It may take time. It takes some people weeks and months before they wake up to the significance of what is going on. They may gamble all that time. They may lie when they give their therapy but so long as they keep attending, hearing what is said and reading the literature, the light will probably dawn sooner or later. Something must already have happened, whether they know it or not, to make them want to keep coming back.

Later we shall be considering stages 2 and 3. They, like stage 1, have various parts, aspects and sub-divisions. Let me repeat, the order is not chronological, there is really only one experience. It has to be described in this way for the benefit of non-gamblers like me who are trying to understand what is going on. It may help some members of Gamblers Anonymous who wish to understand what is happening to them, but it is not necessary for the enjoyment of the experience. Progress is *into* the various aspects of the experience, not *through* them. It was like that when gambling took hold of them. The impact of the 'door', the excitement of the 'room', and the spell it cast, were all experienced at once and then more and more deeply as time went by. Not only that, but, every time the gambler gambled, going round and round with the motion, and every time he trod the fateful circle of deceit, he deepened for himself the impact of the 'door', the grip of the 'room' and the bondage of the 'spell'.

This pattern is repeated in recovery. Those footsteps which took our member past the club and helped tread the message into his brain are symbolic. Group A of experiences, which we have now dealt with, concern re-orientation. Group B is about direction, progress and achievement. Group C is concerned with reflection on the experience of recovery, on its deeper implications and further progress in personal development. Group B is central. It is about the way to recovery and soon we shall be considering the steps by which it is trodden. First, however, we must follow the gambler's wife to Gam-Anon and see what happens there.

Gamblers Anonymous starts to work

The gambling stops. Stress and tension diminish. Refreshed and renewed the gambler will start to lead a new life.

The factors which help him to make that recovery are a sense of:

Welcome – those who have been shunned are welcomed as they are, for what they are. In this way their pretence can cease.

Identification – self-recognition follows when they listen to others who have endured the same experiences. Fears and loneliness disappear.

Hope – others have faced and are overcoming the same problems and suddenly resolutions and decisions are made to seem possible to them once more.

Freedom – nothing is condemned and nothing condoned so that they can clear their conscience with a real confession and release themselves from the past.

Strength – They are infused with new life by other members of the group and are finally able to begin to build a new life for themselves.

7

Please, let it work!

Once her husband has decided to go to Gamblers Anonymous, it is time for our gambler's wife to come to Gam-Anon. She may already have phoned them for support, she may even have been to some meetings. Even if she has (and she would be one of a tiny minority) this occasion will be just as tense, and full of anxiety and desperate hope as if she had only that day, or the night before, made her first call and found when and where the meeting was held.

If it *is* the first time she has made contact with Gam-Anon, she will be wondering what will happen and how she will get on. But whether she has never been before or this is her tenth visit her thoughts will be concentrated mostly on her husband and what will happen to him – that, after all, is what the journey is about. As we know the situation for herself and the children can be improved even while the gambling continues, but to allow the family a proper chance to have a *normal* and happy life, the gambling must stop altogether. So, when she goes to her first Gam-Anon meeting with her husband all her hopes and fears will centre upon the fact that he is going to Gamblers Anonymous. Will that stop his gambling? How can she believe that it will? How dare she *not* hope and try to believe it? She sees him go into his room and, when she goes into her own, her mind is fixed on what he will be like when he comes out. I saw this clearly one night late in 1964, in the eyes of a new Gam-Anon member. To explain what happened, I will have to describe the physical arrangements of the rooms in which we met. We entered Dawson House from Tufton Street and, a few feet on the left, was the Gam-Anon room. On the first landing, with a bow window overlooking the street, was the Gamblers Anonymous room. That evening Gamblers Anonymous had a new member, a man in middle life. I cannot remember if he said much or anything at all, but I knew he had had a long gambling career, that he had five children with an age range of at least ten years, and that if anyone ever looked weary, worn and sad, he did. As it happened, the Gam-Anon meeting concluded first and, when I went downstairs I found myself looking at the Gam-Anon members waiting in the passage below. My attention was drawn to the new Gam-Anon member, with her lifeless, dull hair, and her drawn, lined face. I could never have believed then how those lines would disappear, that hair recover and that face become so much younger and so radiant. Was it in months or years?

Just then, however, my attention was almost entirely drawn to her eyes. They did not see me or anyone else. They were focused only on her husband. They had in them a question which could be expressed in several ways. Was it yes or no? Was it a new life or the same old living death? Were they to return to their soul-destroying misery or were they to be released? She was and is a Catholic, sincere and devout. She believed in miracles but now, she did not know quite what to expect. When he came into view would the halo be in place, would the wings be starting to sprout behind the shoulders? The whole of life depended on what had happened in that room.

Sometimes, of course, the gambler himself will have made the first contact and attended for the first time on his own. His wife may then go with him the following week. In that case, the state of anxiety in which she enters the room will be rather different but it will be just as real.

Can he really change his ways just by meeting a lot of other gamblers? If, as is likely, the gambler's wife has been in touch with some Gam-Anon members during the week, she may have begun to believe that what he told her was true. Still, even though she will be doubtful, this is too important a matter for her to take a wait-and-see attitude.She has to hope.

She is anxious as she enters the room, and probably she experiences other strong emotions as well. She is likely to resent having been made to endure so much as she resents being brought to confess to strangers that her life is in ruins. At the same time she will be concerned for her husband for his own sake. Astonishingly, after everything that has happened, she fears what will become of *him* if he does not change. Don't imagine that I am going to talk of the power of love to survive all circumstances, hate will have too often, too violently, too spontaneously overwhelmed her. She may, even often, have wished him dead. We are now facing the way in which, like it or not, we become deeply involved with those people whose lives are intimately bound up with our own.

Whatever happens, the gambler's wife's life will be affected by his reaction to what he finds in that room. He may settle there at once, but if her husband comes away shrugging or laughing it all off, saying he is not going again, she may feel that it has all ended in nothing and not return herself either. The same thing may happen if her husband returns to gambling after a period (no matter how long) if at the same time he breaks away from Gamblers Anonymous.

We learned earlier that, when he returns to gambling, a gambler finds that all his old thinking returns at once. The impact on his wife must be terrible and I have been told by wives who have experienced this, that, without warning, their old bitter passions and uncontrolled emotions overwhelmed them right away. I have heard this happening when a Gamblers Anonymous member telephoned me as soon as he had gambled again. I knew his wife well and how calm and competent she had become, how whole a person she appeared to be now her husband had stopped gambling. Yet, in the background, I could hear her screaming comments on what he was saying. Members of Gam-Anon discuss the possibility of this happening and if it is at all possible, help each other when it does happen.

No wonder then that the first-time member is anxious and disturbed about the outcome of this evening. Little wonder if, like her husband, she too passes the evening without hearing every word that is spoken. She is also wrapped up in her own affairs. The meeting, however, takes care of that. She is received lovingly and gently into what must seem to be an environment of strength, confidence and security. She must sense that, sooner or later, she will relax here, something she has not done for as long as she can remember.

There are key words here as well. The most important is unity. It expresses the whole purpose, meaning and influence of the meetings. Those who come are intellectually and emotionally in pieces. In their common need, they first find unity as a group. Slowly, their own personal life comes together and, by degrees, they achieve unity with their families and with the world around them.

They can never know for certain how far they have gone with that process. They feel most confident of their personal unity, their oneness with their families and with the world in the unity of the Gam-Anon room. Sitting with them you can feel the soothing of minds, the peace and serenity they share. You can also feel the horizons of your own life extending and begin to think more quietly, more logically and more realistically.

In this room as in the other, a new member is drawn gently in. She is welcomed, recognized by her first name, given a seat and quietly included in the group. The meeting proceeds around her in much the same way as it does in Gamblers Anonymous, though there are variations in form and atmosphere. That is understandable, the groups represent opposite sides of the same problem. Passages are read from a number of different books and members speak in turn of their own experiences. They raise matters which are, for them, immediate problems which have to be dealt with. One may be experiencing a crisis of some kind with her gambler and she may need help to do the right thing. Perhaps, while the gambling continued she had to take the entire responsibility for their children and the home. The recovering gambler begins to take an interest in these things for the first time and has his own ideas about the way things should work. Having had to cope alone it is difficult for her to relax her hold and accept his involvement, even when it is beneficial. This creates tension, from which she needs to find a release.

Another may speak of her children's problems, telling the group how their lives and personalities have been adversely affected over the years. Financial difficulties are frequently discussed – they happen no matter what care is taken to avoid them – as are the difficulties members have with themselves and their emotions. When it is appropriate, members comment on what has been said. They do not give advice though they may make suggestions – although each understands from experience what the other is talking about, personalities and circumstances differ greatly and one may achieve what another cannot.

Because her situation is considered from several points of view, the original speaker is able to see her own life from a variety of perspectives. She may or may not yet see a solution, and even if she does, she may not think she can put it into practice, at least not for the time being. However, even if she is going back to live with the problem, she will now be able to think around it, and will not feel the same sense of defeat.

The new Gam-Anon member recognizes that the existing members share her problems, but they are dealing with them with a confidence and competence she could not have imagined possible. She identifies with them and is aware of seeing herself in them. This quietens her, she *has* found the right place. Also, she learns that even the worst gambler can stop gambling and that most, if not all, of the partners of the women in the room, have done so. All this fortifies her. She is able to relax a little, searching the faces of the women around her and trying to explore their minds. She may or may not speak that first evening with words of her own but over the months and years to come she will say a good deal in that room. Like her partner, she will speak for her own sake. She will speak what must be spoken. Her statements, too, are therapeutic.

When she does speak she will be relieved that she can adopt the form of identification used by the other members. She gives her first name and adds, 'I am the wife (or any other description she wants to use) of a compulsive gambler'. In using that expression she has explained what she is and why she is so. She is like a tree whose growth has been blocked and has twisted this way and that when unable to grow upwards. It is distorted, not by nature, but by circumstances and so is she. She is the 'wife' of a compulsive gambler. What she does not know yet is that the time will come when she can acknowledge her status with gratitude. Those who succeed in making a recovery in Gam-Anon recognize that their suffering and their release from it have enriched them. They can better understand human frailty, believe in the good in the worst of people, and know an experience of forgiveness so effective that its capacity for changing and restoring lives seems unlimited. They have plumbed the depths and survived. They are wives of compulsive gamblers. Even the friends of compulsive gamblers and of their wives can share that experience.

When she speaks, this wife of a compulsive gambler will have a lot to talk about. The order in which we speak of her themes will not, perhaps, be the most logical.

First, and it may surprise her when she realizes it, she has much to confess. She may never have seen herself as an offender, only as one much offended against. Time and the meeting itself will bring her to a more complete understanding of her situation. She may be troubled most by recollections of the way she has mistreated her children. She needs to consider how this situation has changed – how she is making amends – perhaps simply because she has become a different person, a new mother, living a different life. She will also need to find out what special help her children should have to allow them to recover fully from the effects of the difficult period they have lived through. But most of all, the wife or partner of a compulsive gambler needs to be reconciled to herself. This process begins when she talks to other people about her experience. As well as mistreating her children, she has treated others in a manner which she is now ashamed of. However, it is more than a matter of words and actions, the depths to which she had sunk in her thoughts now frightens her. Once the need to purge herself of these experiences is being met, she can at last begin to see that all this played a large part in reducing her to her present condition.

In this room she can work out all her feelings of anger, humiliation and shame because the others will take it. They know. They have been there. They understand how the terrible things she describes could happen. Indeed, how they are inevitable. As she talks she begins to see what she did and said in the context of the life she was living and to see things in proportion. She begins to accept herself. She enjoys relief and finds peace. Some hurt remains, but the wounds heal and she can and does forgive herself.

There is often a burden of guilt from which she must find release. There is no real reason for her guilt, it is part of the state of mind to which she has become a victim. She feels guilty because her husband is a gambler, even taking responsibility either for his gambling or for the lengths to which he takes it. She feels guilty about the shortcomings of her home and of the life her family endures. Sometimes she just feels guilty. Her husband often encourages this feeling in her, working on it and using it for his own ends. Every time a problem comes up, he throws the blame for everything upon her. She has to talk this out, until the burden is gone.

As well as guilt she will invariably feel shame. One of the earliest members of Gam-Anon in the UK still remembers well the relief she felt when she realized that she could invite the other members to her home. For years she had felt unable to invite anyone there because she was so ashamed of it. At last there were others with neglected homes – and people she was proud to know. The deepest shame a gambler's wife feels, though, is shadowy, shapeless, and pervasive. It is the kind of shame we feel if a relation, a close friend or associate, or an organization with which we are involved, does wrong or comes under suspicion. We are sensitive about our reputations. Because, occasionally, she sees a bank statement, a building society account, and because some people call or telephone about debts, she knows there is trouble for herself and her family out there in the world. Because she does not know the whole story and cannot get the truth from her husband her imagination fills in the gaps. She imagines people pointing her out, whispering and wagging their heads and that eats away inside her. One member said she stopped going out altogether. She hung her washing on the line at night and if she walked into the front room during the day she crept along the walls or ducked under the window ledge so as not to be seen. This, too, has to be confronted at the meeting, talked out and overcome, so that she knows that she can, and must, hold up her head and recover her old confidence.

Now we turn to her basic therapy, her account of her life as the wife of a compulsive gambler. Much of what she says will cover the same ground as her husband's therapy though the stories will not fit each other as precisely as two parts of one whole might be expected to do. He speaks of what he did, she of what she suffered. Each sees it from their own point of view and speaks from his or her experience.

There are at least three reasons why she needs to tell her story. The first is because she is a human being with natural feelings and has been hurt. She needs to be heard and understood. For years she has been unable to confide in anyone. If she has tried to do so, no matter to whom she speaks, people are likely to be embarrassed, abuse her husband or call her a fool. But now, the quiet understanding of her new friends enables her to lay it out, event by event, see it all objectively and look at it constructively. As she describes the blow that beat her to her knees, she begins to feel that, sooner or later, she will be able to stand up again.

The second reason she has to tell this story is that she needs to release the resentment, anger, bitterness, hatred, scorn, and jealousy of others that have become natural to her, indeed, essential to her self-defence. They have harmed her, though. Every time she discharged them on her husband, on her children, relatives, neighbours, workmates, the world in general, the result has only been more humiliation and more self-disgust. She must free herself of them to recover. In this room she can say what she really feels, and not need to waste the words in abusing her partner or trying simply to get things off her chest for a while. Instead she can use them to purge herself of the poison gambling has put in her soul. She can do this in this room because here her words are received by understanding and sympathetic minds. You can only rid yourself of emotions like these when they are taken from you.

The third reason why a gambler's wife has to tell this story is that she must get to the bottom of why it is that, as the wife of a compulsive gambler, she had to suffer all these things, why he had to do it all to her. What is this business of being a compulsive gambler? What was going on inside him? If she is told, and roughly this is what she will be told, that he was sick and could not help doing what he did, how can she hope that he will be able to behave differently in the future? Well, there will be no future if she does not understand what made him what he was, and that he can change and that she will never reach that understanding until the hurt, anger and resentment through which she sees him are cleared away.

There is more to it than that though. She needs to understand because she has some big decisions to make. She has to know what chance there is that her husband will stop gambling, how sure she can be that he will be a different person. She has to understand what their life together will be like, once her husband has stopped gambling. She needs to know all this because she has to decide whether or not to continue the relationship and, if she does, on what terms. Even if later she decides to separate from her husband, this experience of understanding and forgiving herself and him will not have been wasted. Unless she goes through it, the hurt, anger and resentment will remain and spoil her future.

Now, these two people have to achieve their recovery and, important as the meetings are, that is done in the home and in the world. Helped by the guidance and encouragement they are given, they begin from the first evening and, apart from being 'in GA' and 'in Gam-Anon', they do it on their own. Fortunately there is a way to follow and it is that way which we will now consider.

Gam-Anon releases partners of problem gamblers from:

- their frozen state of tense and knotted anxiety
- their crippling sense of defeat
- the sick condition of false guilt
- the sick condition of false shame

Gam-Anon gives its members:

- **unity** – in the group, within themselves and with life
- peace, serenity, hope, confidence and laughter
- the chance to talk problems over
- the chance to find release from proper guilt and shame
- the chance to feel understood
- the chance to release pent-up emotions
- the chance to find the meaning of what happened to them and why
- the chance to find their feet and decide about their lives
- the renewed ability to integrate with others

8

The way to recovery

In this chapter, we follow the gambler as he is put on the way to recovery, and as he treads it with his wife. He knows what he wants – a normal life. Most of all he wants an ordinary domestic routine, a set pattern to follow from the moment he wakes up in the morning. Many of the people I met in my office on their way to Gamblers Anonymous expressed this clearly. They wanted just to wake up, get up, wash, shave, dress, have their breakfast and go to work. They wanted to stop waking up to a kind of nightmare, the brain already scheming about the day's gambling and where to get the money for their next stake.

Some readers may find it hard to believe that the compulsive gambler just wants peace and quiet. How will he get on without the gambling? Won't he want that stimulation? Surely what he wants is not peace and quiet at all, but to have all the excitement of gambling without any of the problems? While the assumption that all potential problem gamblers have an above average need for stimulation fits in with a certain understanding of addictions – those who become addicted have a deep, unmet need which is fulfilled only when they find the substance or activity to which they have become addicted – there is an error at the heart of this theory. In my view, the belief that the appeal of, for instance, 'action' gambling, is negative is misguided. As I said before my observation of compulsive gamblers leads me to believe that the appeal 'action' gambling has is positive. People are drawn to it, even those who lead very full lives. It is a seducer rather than a pit. Of course, arousal and stimulation are a fundamental part of this appeal and those who are able to be 'carried away' by it must find it enjoyable but that is not to say that they would not be relieved to be without it. Of course, for some time after they have given it up, their jangled nerves will continue to cry out for the 'action' but this is a withdrawal symptom, not a measure of a fundamental need for excessive stimulation.

Problem gamblers vary in this matter as in others. As they recover, they tend to find the level of stimulation they need in their careers and leisure interests. Some really do enjoy a quiet life. In any case, when problem gamblers know they want to stop it is because the gambling has raised the level of stimulation in their lives to the point where it is unbearable. They cannot bear to gamble with their lives any longer. Twenty-four hours' tension is too much, they want to escape from torment, they want to stop and relax into a normal life. Joining Gamblers Anonymous is obviously the first crucial step, but there is still a long way to go before true peace of mind can be achieved. Now our gambler is in a double turmoil – his mind is in tumult and so is his life. To achieve a return to normality both he and his life must change. What Gamblers Anonymous tells him is that if he sets about controlling the turmoil in his life, he will find the turmoil in his mind calming down of its own accord.

The way to recovery is composed of a number of practical actions. Each one of a member's many problems has to be tackled and dealt with. Emphasis is put on telling the truth and taking responsible actions. It is an effort at first, but, like learning and practising a new skill, it becomes easier as time goes by, members become more honest and more responsible. They are 'putting on' the person they once were. We should not be surprised that inward change follows and depends upon outward change. A problem gambler became what he is now in much the same way. Gambling was his goal and the way he pursued it led him to take actions which corrupted his mind. The way in was devious; the way back is straight.

His new friends point him to that way. It is signposted and marked out in steps. For this middle stage of recovery the key word of Gamblers Anonymous in the United States may help us. Instead of talking about being 'in GA' they speak of being 'on the program'. There is a recovery programme and, provided the group is on form and the turmoil in his mind allows it, the new member will be put on to it that very night. If those conditions do not prevail he may well miss out. It is hardest for the group to make a sufficient impact on a new member if it only consists of very few members. If only one member is present, the difficulties are considerable. Quite simply, new members of any organization like to be lost in the crowd until they find their bearings. Also, a single existing member has to make so direct an 'attack' on a new one that he is in great danger of frightening him away.

Still, numbers are not everything, and even large groups will not always be on form. Any Gamblers Anonymous group is composed of recovering compulsive gamblers, each in the process of regaining stability and maturity. The group is not there for the new member alone. It is *not* a clinic, and the new member is *not* a patient. It is a tightly knit unit bound together by a common need, hope, and effort. Each one is there for himself, but he throws in his lot with the others because he depends upon them. Even when a new member is present, the existing members must still deal with their own problems. Every meeting counts for people who are fighting a desperate day-to-day battle.

The new member has to 'get into the act' just as, when he was gambling, he got into the 'action' of that. He does so by responding to what the existing members are saying and doing about themselves. In a way, it is a bit like catching a train. The new member is given an opportunity to join, but the train does not stop for long in the station. He has to jump on board while he's got the chance and go with his fellow members. Fortunately for him, one of the steps in the Recovery Programme asking members to 'carry the message' to those who still suffer, is taken very seriously. What is more, the existing members need him, particularly those who have been there longest and may be in danger of becoming complacent. His presence reminds them of what they once were. So they make a place for him in the circle and do their best to get through to him while dealing with their own affairs.

The new member's state of mind, more than anything else, is likely to block out the message. He may hear nothing and his problems will still be racing around inside his head. His armoury of responses is ready, the instant 'explanation', the immediate self-justification, the reflex angry rejoinder, the swift flight from the scene, the spontaneous escape to the 'action' in which he seeks oblivion. He is an experienced con-man, a thoroughgoing manipulator, and he cannot enter the room in any other frame of mind. Deep within, though, he is alone and frightened.

He may not like what he hears. He brings with him gambling and problems and he may hope to keep gambling but get rid of his problems. When he finds that he is expected to give up gambling *and* keep the problems, why should he be interested? Members of Gamblers Anonymous no doubt get it right in some cases when they say that those who do not return need to suffer much more before they are ready to stop. This is not true in every case, though, as I shall discuss further later.

The first step the recovering gambler has to take is to give a positive answer to the question, 'Do you want to stop gambling?' This means: 'You ask for help, but are you serious about it?' That desire is the single requirement for membership of Gamblers Anonymous. The question may not get through first time round or he may not be able to say yes to it. Obsession with his problems can block his mind. One man said he often wanted to stop gambling, 'but how could I? I owed all that money.' However, that all-important 'yes' is the essential starting point for recovery. If the gambler doesn't want to stop, there is little point in going on.

If the meeting is on form, and if the new member stays behind, one or two members will take him on one side and guide him towards the next step, which is to see that his problem is not money but gambling. He may resist that. If he does, they will ply him with questions. Does he ever win? Does he ever win enough to pay off his debts or at least the most pressing ones? The answers are yes. Does he actually pay any debts off? The answer is no, unless someone is right on his tail. What does he do with the money? He admits that what he wins is gambling money. It is sacred for that purpose. It is not to be used to pay debts or support the home. So what happens in the end? He loses, he always loses. It may be the same day, the next day or a few days later, but he always loses, the money always goes back.

Then what does he do? He gets hold of more money to try to win back what he has lost. Then what happens? He loses again. In the end, he admits that gambling has taken him deeper and deeper into debt and into all kinds of problems and never could get him out of any of them. His problem *is* gambling, not money, and once he has seen that he is ready for the next step: he must not gamble tomorrow. That is not a moral injunction, Gamblers Anonymous does not take a moral stance towards gambling. He needs to stop, and if he is to do so he must do it *now*, by accepting that he has had his last bet and resolving that he will not gamble tomorrow.

Yes, just tomorrow. Always a resolve at night not to gamble tomorrow, and renew your resolution every morning, 'I will not gamble today.' Take it one day at a time, just for today. Step by step this will take you through the program, see you on the way. By doing this the gambler is already curbing his impatience and controlling his dream world, making decisions about what he will not do.

If these members are on their toes they will now find out if he needs to take emergency action about his debts – for example he may be expecting a court summons or his house may be about to be repossessed. If this proves to be so he will be advised to face up to his problems and not to try to run away from them. They won't moralize, but they are anxious about him. They know that prison or other punishment will not of itself do any good, but they also know that running away leads to more gambling, further crime and greater trouble. Recovery from compulsive gambling comes by facing up to things and taking the consequences. The way to the police station can be a step on the way to recovery and if he goes, Gamblers Anonymous will go with him.

The compulsive gambler may also feel under threat at work – perhaps he has been embezzling or spending time gambling when he should have been working. For the same reasons, he will be recommended to face up to the situation. The other members of GA will seek to understand this as fully as possible, and try to find some way in which the gambler can keep his job while still being open about everything. But even if he has to lose his job and go to prison he will have started his recovery.

Members may go to court to speak on behalf of another but over the years Gamblers Anonymous has become cautious about this. Their intervention can lead to a reduced sentence, but the result can be a sigh of relief and a return to gambling. Nowadays such appearances are generally limited to those cases where members have proved their sincerity and commitment to stopping gambling over the course of a number of meetings, perhaps when they were on bail awaiting trial or sentence.

The new member's mind will be full of problems other than money or an imminent court case, but it is not time yet to deal with these. The one remaining thing to be asked on the first night is: 'Does your wife (your husband, your parents) know everything?' The answer is almost always no. The advice he will receive in return which is almost a command, so important is the matter, is, 'You must tell her everything.'

This is never easy. Many people's first reaction is that it is impossible, they think she could not take it. Indeed, they may have come (or allowed themselves to be brought) to the GA meeting because they hoped somehow to avoid telling her. Some say she is just back from hospital after having a nervous or mental breakdown and could not stand the shock. Others say that she has threatened to leave or throw them out if they gambled again and they are sure she will do it if she finds out.

Difficult though it is, she must be told. It may not be done that night, but unless it is done, and soon, there is no hope of the problem gambler making a recovery. He gambled in secret. Indeed, it was fundamental to that way of life that everything was secret. He cannot, however, recover in secret, not least because he will need his wife's co-operation. In future, she will be affected by everything he does and will be involved in a great deal of it, so unless everything is now open and above board, he can go no further.

This step, too, gives him a new experience. To deceive her, he had to shut himself off from her. To explain things to her, he has to open himself up to her. He may start to realize how he subjected her to fear and uncertainty, how much she needs to know what he has to say, how glad she is to hear it.

When she can say, 'Is that all?' and start to believe that it is, she knows she will begin to feel her feet on the ground again. It is better to know about thousands of pounds of debt than to be in fear about what you think must be at least hundreds.

Next the new member must deal with his financial situation. A 'pressure' group should be formed to help him. When, from his New York experience, Henry said, 'We set up a pressure group', I thought of the English Court of the Star Chamber and the Spanish Inquisition. However, as he explained, the purpose is not to put pressure on members but to relieve them of pressures that could cause them to revert to gambling. One evening, then, preferably in his own home, with his wife and one or more experienced members of Gamblers Anonymous, the recovering gambler will have to make a list of all his creditors. This can be almost physically painful: he has consistently tried to forget them and been bothered by his debts only when creditors have bothered him, but he is given time and questions help probe his memory. Nothing must be missed, nothing may be ignored no matter how insignificant it appears or how shameful. If a debt is undeclared, it is like a land-mine for the gambler. When it eventually comes to light it can revive his guilty fears, his tendency to panic, his devious thinking and will almost certainly prompt him to start gambling again.

Once a complete list of debts has been compiled, a provisional plan for repaying them in weekly or monthly instalments is drawn up. Priority must be given to those debts which can put the family security at risk: the rent, the mortgage repayments, the gas and electricity bills, and the money owed to those who have taken out court orders.

The next question is to find out how much money the family needs to keep itself fed, clothed and housed. The gambler may well not have any idea about this – he has long tried to ignore these matters. His wife will have to take over but the gambler must be involved and take his share of the responsibility, especially when hard decisions have to be arrived at or choices made. The provisional total for payment of debts must be added to this and a margin left for contingencies and for recreation.

The gambler then has to set his budgeted expenditure against his income. It may not be sufficient to meet it so he will either have to revise his budget or, better, increase his income. Members of Gamblers Anonymous often add an early morning, evening or weekend job to their regular work. Most members, anyway, soon improve their financial position by getting promotion or by starting up or rebuilding their own business. Their impatience and imagination, characteristics which helped to destroy them, now work for them.

Writing these lists and deciding on or agreeing to each figure is much more than simply a way of putting the gambler's financial position to rights. Something happens inside him. He starts to engage in discussion. He is forced to be realistic, to be patient and take the long-term view, to be responsible, and to co-operate. Has he really changed? Who can tell? Still he does appear to be heading off in a new direction – he's already beginning to act differently – and that exercises him inwardly just as unaccustomed physical activity would stretch his muscles.

The next step will exercise him even more. The time has come when he must contact his creditors, put the situation to them and obtain their agreement to his scheme. This introduces him to humility and gives him practice in being honest. The gambler may not know he is experiencing humility. He may only know that he feels bad when he tells each creditor how he has gambled himself to ruin, and how good he feels when he has done it. He may not yet recognize that he is adjusting himself to life, but that is what he is doing. In the same way, he experiences honesty as he tells the truth. It cannot be otherwise. In chapter 2 we saw how the need to get money for gambling led him to deceive himself and others until, as Gamblers Anonymous says, he became a compulsive liar as well as a compulsive gambler. Now, his need to recover is forcing him to tell the truth. No one can yet say that he is honest – he will wrestle with his character change for a long while yet.

Still, it is a considerable step to recognize the practical value of honesty. In the early autumn of 1964 a man who had attended for about six weeks, burst out in his therapy: 'I tell you, honesty is the best policy.' After refusing to do so for several weeks he had met one of his creditors. It happened at his house and Henry, the American

GA member, had been there as well. The scene was graphically
described, his right forefinger jabbing in each direction as he spoke.
'He (the creditor) sat there, Henry there, my wife and I there. I said
to him, "I done your money and my money, gambling". He said,
"You done what?" I said, "I done your money and my money,
gambling." Then Henry told him about GA and how I would pay
back bit by bit, and he began to assure Henry that I am a good
worker and can earn the money to pay him back – as if I owed the
money to Henry and not to him! I tell you,' he reiterated, 'honesty
is the best policy.' The impact of this on the rest of the group was
tremendous, not least on me. This man, in his fifties, was just learning that honesty is the best policy. I had learnt that before I was five.
If I confessed, people often let the thing pass. If I waited to be found
out, I was punished. This is practical wisdom, not morality.

You see people change at this stage in their recovery. In the same
autumn another man, accompanied by his wife, spent their two
weeks' holiday meeting creditors. They told me about it afterwards,
standing together, so much a couple, looking so alive, so relieved, so
happy – yet about £15,000 in debt. They have never looked back.

In fact, most members' creditors surprised and impressed me, they
were sympathetic and constructive. No doubt they were glad to get
their money back but many said, 'Can you afford so much?' others,
'I am glad about this. I didn't know what was wrong but I am happy
that you are putting it right.' How do they know he is telling the
truth? Well, the fact is, they don't, but what the gambler is saying
is so uncharacteristic that they take it at face value and test the truth
as the instalments come. Some members need moral support when
they go to face their creditors. On one occasion, I found myself with
a new member outside his bank manager's door. He said he was
shaking with nerves. Previously, with well-spun yarns at the ready
and determined to get a further loan, he had felt confident. Now,
having to tell the truth, he felt vulnerable and exposed.

At this stage it is all still heady and exhilarating stuff. The family's
life is being turned around. Its members are being drawn together,
man and wife are sharing a common purpose and common action.
There is a honeymoon period. But then comes the long, arduous
journey down the way to recovery. It is trodden step by step.
Another day, another week, another month, without a gamble. The
weekly or monthly payments are steadily made and the balanced and
budgeted life progresses. They are on the program, treading the way
to recovery, man, wife and children together. Being 'in GA' and 'in
Gam-Anon' becomes more and more essential – the weekly 'shot in

the arm' to keep them going. There is a light at the end of the tunnel which becomes steadily brighter and draws them on. Their tangled lives are beginning to unravel and the partnership is becoming closer.

Do not be deceived, though, getting back together is not easy. The peace that settles between the problem gambler and his family is a fragile one – especially when each partner has a long way to go towards becoming a 'nice' person again. The difficulties they suffer are a legacy of the past. For instance, the wife will be trying to recover trust while the gambler is trying to tell the truth. Only his persistent truthfulness can restore the trust they once had but in the meantime he needs to be believed. Why can't she believe him when he is telling the truth? When he explains something she has to calm her agitation and control her reflex response: 'Has he?', 'Did he?', 'Was he?' and bite back the words: 'Have you?', 'Did you?', 'Were you?' He has to catch his slick mind in the act as it slides along well-worn grooves to produce an 'instant truth'.

Each side has to do something positive. Once again, it is a matter of control. The gambling partner must make himself realize how difficult it is for his wife to trust him and, for both their sakes, he must slow down his reactions, take time to think before he speaks, and make sure he does present the truth. This does take time and a lot of effort.

On the wife's side, she must try to notice the facts of the new life rather than interpret everything through her fears. He is not gambling or stealing. He is more reliable and takes more responsibility. Even so, recovering trust is a question of healing a wound and that won't happen quickly. It happens, though. His withdrawal symptoms make things even harder. He is restless, impatient, irritable, bad tempered, but remember, changing your life is traumatic. When newer members ask what will replace gambling in their lives, they are not just thinking of alternative activities. Gambling was their *total* life, dominating them at all times. Stress and tension remain, nerves continue to jangle, abused and damaged emotions cry out for the 'action' which has suddenly ceased. They cannot sit still. This is their problem, of course, and they must deal with it and see it through in the best way they can. Unjust though it is, those who previously suffered at their hands are now called upon to exercise patience.

While this lasts, recovering gamblers may feel the need to make excessive use of alcohol and tobacco, even of drugs in order to control their emotions, just as they did while gambling. From the first I recognized how necessary a cigarette was to most members when they came to give their therapy. Immediately before or after giving

their name and saying, '. . . and I am a compulsive gambler', they
would light a cigarette, inhale deeply, and then speak. Of course, as
time passed, the *need* to smoke would decline along with stress and
tension.

There are dangers. The old ways can insinuate themselves into
new situations. One man, an insurance agent, had, in his gambling
days, always gambled the premiums he collected as he collected them
in cash during the week. He would settle at the office by cheque on
Thursday. On Friday, he would race round to collect enough of next
week's money to cover the cheque before it was cleared. When settling with his creditors, his impatience and dream world imagination
led him to overstretch himself and once again he found that he was
getting in next week's money to pay this week's instalments. Obviously, it could not last. Eventually, he had to change to a job where
he did not handle money and re-negotiate his scheme of repayments
with his creditors. In doing this he made real progress in recovery.
Another man, also driven by his impatience, undertook both an early morning and a weekend job to supplement the income from his
daily work so that he could clear his debts more quickly. At the same
time, he seemed to transfer his 'compulsion' from gambling to
Gamblers Anonymous. He travelled to three meetings a week, all
many miles from his home. One was his own group and he went to
the others to provide much-needed inspiration and support. He still
appeared to be living on adrenalin and gambled after twenty months'
abstention.

Yet another man, self-employed and needing to earn a good income to pay his debts and maintain his wife and son, was so carried
away by enthusiasm for the honorary duties he had undertaken on
behalf of Gamblers Anonymous that he neglected his work almost
to the point of disaster. His wife naturally protested strongly and
their marriage was threatened. Some years after that a man in a
similar situation realized that he must resign his voluntary national
office in Gamblers Anonymous at once, well before his period of service ended. In a general letter to the fellowship he said:

> '. . . *during the past eighteen months I have seen a steady deterioration
> in my marriage, my work and myself, and I believe that immediate
> remedial action is necessary if I am to avoid ending up in the Divorce
> Court, the dole queue and the betting shop. My problem stems from the
> fact that I have unwittingly switched my gambling compulsion to a
> compulsion for GA . . . and the result is that my life is more precarious
> than when I first entered GA over six years ago. No employer or wife*

would accept the treatment I have been dishing out over the past couple of years. I've "stolen" a hundred days' sick leave besides having developed an appalling attitude towards my job and, although I met and married my wife after I had given up gambling, she certainly knows what it is like to live with a compulsive person.'

Even if these difficulties are avoided, the gambler still has a tough fight on his hands to make the break with his old way of life, and he will have to struggle harder to overcome the fear and loneliness which used to make him run to hide in a gambling environment. When a new member says with pride, 'I have not gambled for a week', the veterans know how much that means. But what about a month or a year with no gambling? The first year is the hardest and longest, full of tense relationships made tenser by the need to watch every penny and to maintain rigorous self-control. The achievement brings a warrior's triumph.

It is tough and new members are urged to attend as many meetings as possible. Frequent attendance does make it easier to stay 'in GA'. They are advised to take the handbook given to them at their first meeting everywhere and read it when they can. Its message will help them and it forms a link with the meeting. Existing members will telephone new members (in both GA and Gam-Anon) between meetings. As soon as they are seen to be taking recovery seriously they will be given a telephone list and encouraged to make calls themselves. Ideally, a new member will be given a sponsor to whom he can go for advice and help, but this is a personal arrangement, and one that it is not always possible to make. Sometimes new members 'appoint' and use their own sponsor. However it is done, they must stay 'in GA' or they will not stay on the program. Members with ten years and more of non-gambling behind them say that without the meetings and the literature they fear they would gamble again.

Progress comes as members adjust to the facts of life. One member of twelve weeks described how he had been welcomed each Friday when he took home his pay. He received a loving kiss, his warmed slippers and his dinner. He basked in it and felt a hero. One Friday, however, his wife seized the money as he entered the door and rush-ed off to buy something. He felt lost. Then it hit him. What he had done was really nothing more than any man would do at the end of the week. He was not a hero.

Couples have to decide between them how they are going to manage their money. There is no rule, but in practice the wife generally looks after it. Most recovering gamblers are happy to have with them only the money they need to cover daily expenses. Having more than that might well encourage them to return to gambling. So wives settle the bills. Even so the gambler takes his share, perhaps a leading one, in deciding how the money should be spent. All this has to be worked out in life but, as one wife told me, the meetings help them to do it better. Therapies undergo a change. The past is examined with greater sensitivity and deeper insight. Present changes in life are described. Everyday problems are met and overcome. There is no longer a need to escape in gambling.

All this is achieved as the problem gambler moves along the road to solvency. The total amount owed gets smaller each week or month confirming the sense of achievement, with each debt cleared representing another milestone passed. There is that great occasion, too, when the GA member is awarded his first year pin. The little gold lapel pin bears the initials GA and a number, from one to five, to indicate the total of gambling-free years. The five year pin is replaced at ten, 15 and 20 years. Intervening 'birthdays' are simply recognized without a change of pin. It is the GA member's pin but wives share in the occasion fully. They usually present the pin and receive flowers from their Gam-Anon friends.

It is a time of joy for husband and wife. They have done more than improve their financial position. They have grown together and experienced the re-birth of respect. Self-respect has to come first to give the word meaning but respect for the changing partner will follow hard on its heels. Respect for and of the children is also important. Together the gambler and his wife learn respect for their family and friends, for other people in general, and for life itself and are much moved when others respect them in return. The pin signifies all this and more besides.

There are times of danger. The first Christmas, when there is not much money for celebration, is one. Every year, there is a temptation to gamble to try to make enough out of a little. Some succumb although those that talk about it to their family find that this can help them over the difficult period they are now facing.

Don't think problem gamblers are weak people, though. You have to be strong to battle against your weakness. Impatience and the dream world are second nature to them and are the things that brought them down but they can rise again when, contrary to their nature, they adopt patience and realism, consider things from all angles and look ahead before making decisions.

Some consider solvency their goal and, having stopped gambling and saved the money to clear their debts, they will leave. In doing so they miss certain deeper changes which we shall look at in more detail in chapter 14. Now though we must turn our attention to the fact that at least one in four of those who come through the door of the GA room do not return the following week; perhaps they will make contact again some years later, perhaps never.

The Gambler's recovery – from turmoil to an ordered life

The rule: change the actions and the personality will change. There are certain practical steps which must be taken on the way to recovery:

- accepting that gambling must stop (admitting that he was wrong)

- recognizing that the problem is gambling, not money (a return to realism)

- making the decision night by night not to gamble tomorrow, day by day not to gamble today (curbing impatience, controlling the dream world)

- if it applies, facing the police and/or his employer (taking the consequences of his actions instead of avoiding them)

- telling the family everything (renewing relationships)

- facing the domestic financial situation with the family (learning to co-operate)

- facing and coming to agreement with creditors (practising humility and honesty)

- patiently acting honestly while waiting for trust in him to return

- enduring and controlling the effect of withdrawal symptoms – restlessness, impatience, irritability, bad temper

- being continually vigilant in case the dream world and impatience lead him back to gambling or to other follies or excesses

- keeping up with repayments of debts week after week or month after month for years

- making sure that every opportunity which the new life presents is enjoyed to the full and recognizing its rewards

- enjoying the renewed ability to give and receive respect

9
Help from the caring agencies

Gamblers Anonymous and Gam-Anon give so much to so many, that it is no reflection on them to say that they cannot help everyone who comes to them and that some of those they do help need additional assistance. There is, therefore, a part to be played by academic researchers and the caring professions. We shall be considering what that is in this chapter.

There is a specific reason why it is necessary to consider the help other professional individuals and agencies can offer compulsive gamblers. The general experience of GA groups throughout the UK and over the years is that they retain only one in four, or 25 per cent, of all new arrivals long enough for them to set out on a programme of recovery. Those who may be said to constitute this 'norm' for Gamblers Anonymous will be considered further on page 88. The remaining 75 per cent fall into three categories. The first are those who lose touch almost immediately, often not even returning for a second visit. The second are individuals who attend for weeks, maybe even months and appear to be fitting quite well into the life of the group, however, they leave within a year – well before their recovery is consolidated. The final category – a significant minority – attending for years, alternate between periods of abstinence and periods of gambling. Some eventually pull through but there are others who do not.

Gamblers Anonymous takes this matter of retention seriously. The subject of the retention of members appears frequently on the agendas of regional and national committees and of national and international conventions. However, in spite of this, the situation does not alter much from year to year and for some time now I have been of the opinion that many of those who fall into one of the three categories mentioned above need either additional or alternative help of the kind that the caring agencies can give.

As far as the first category of 'leavers' is concerned, it is important to recognize that it is a matter of touch and go as to whether new members are retained from the first night. Reference has already been made to this problem in chapter 6, and again in chapter 8 where the theme was developed. We must now, as we promised then, consider the case of those whom Gamblers Anonymous does not manage to hold onto, but who none the less, are still seriously seeking help to stop gambling.

Quite a few of these, I am sure, do not return simply because this is not the place for them. In no way can Gamblers Anonymous be blamed for this. It is just that human beings vary in nature and temperament so that, as in most things, what works for one individual may not necessarily suit another. I can understand that some people might find a Gamblers Anonymous meeting too much of a shock. Not everyone can feel at home in such an intimate, frank and forceful unit. Not everyone is able to speak intimately about themselves in front of a group of people. Some find it disturbing rather than helpful when those around them bare their souls. Such people may feel more secure in the confidential and personal environment which the caring professions can provide.

Let us now consider the second type of 'leaver', the one who does return after the first meeting and for weeks or months after, fitting quite happily into the life of the group but who leaves before his first year of membership is out. These members are the ones who have difficulty in summoning up the will to stop gambling and to stay away from it. It is very tempting to blame their lapse on the fact that they do not really *want* to stop but I don't think it would be fair to do so. Gamblers Anonymous demands a great deal of its members. At that first meeting the gambler will have to resolve not to gamble tomorrow. He will then have to keep that resolve alive and carry it through successfully for a whole week until the next meeting, usually in the face of great stress and temptation. This is a way which only the thoroughly desperate and the heroic will dare to tread. It demands that people go against their own nature, that with patience and realism they climb, slowly but consistently, up the hill down which their natural impatience and dream world impelled them. It is a way that strips them of their protective fantasies and confronts them with their own self-inflicted failure and loss. It is a way that forces them to make a decision to deny the self that was, and to endure anything that is necessary in order to find the self that is to be, even if they have to renew that resolution hour by hour and day by day to do so.

I wonder if anyone, on the basis of a cool decision and relying on willpower alone, would be able to stay the course? Fortunately those who join Gamblers Anonymous do not have to face things on their own. They have the support of many others who have gone through the same experience themselves. From meeting to meeting, they are 'in GA' and they come back time and time again to get their batteries recharged.

Suppose, however, that there came a day when this stopped working for you? Suppose that on a particular day you were confronted by your whole life's problem and whilst in that frame of mind you heard the racing commentary from a betting office or the musical sounds of a gambling machine? What if try as you might, you found, over a period, you could resist temptation only for so long?

One young man put this very problem to me several years ago. I advised him to continue attending Gamblers Anonymous but to seek alternative help through a counsellor or a therapist at the same time. I suggested that a member of a caring agency might well be able to help him put his finger on a hidden and unsuspected factor which was undermining his resolution. They would perhaps be able to help him evolve strategies for getting through each day, ways of handling the problem one day at a time. There is no guarantee that such a course of action would work in every case but it might and for that reason alone it is worth trying.

Others who leave within the first year have additional personal problems which have hampered their recovery, throwing them off balance and prompting a return to gambling. Some who are badly affected in this way just cannot find help in Gamblers Anonymous. For months they endure under great stress, struggling to get on to the way to recovery. If they do manage to stop gambling, it is only for brief periods. They seem never to be able to find any peace within themselves either in 'the room' or outside it. They are generally convinced, and probably with good reason, that outside pressures are driving them back to their old way of life. They resent it when they are told, by people they think are wearing haloes and who seem to be preaching at them, that they gamble only because they want to.

I vividly remember the case of one man whose life was clearly disturbed by a variety of problems. During his therapy it became clear that at any time, any one of them could quite easily upset the fragile balance he had built up and throw his affairs back into disarray. He was separated from his wife and he told us despondently about a visit his daughter had paid him the previous weekend. As usual he had made great plans for entertaining her but, not just as the result of gambling, they had gone awry. The experience had left him feeling humiliated and at odds with himself and he was obviously very close to sliding back into his old ways in an attempt to escape from his shame and distress.

Over the years such additional problems usually become intertwined with the gambling, each exacerbating the other. The help of a professional therapist or counsellor will be necessary in order to disentangle and deal with them.

Finally, we have to consider those members who alternate between periods of abstinence and periods of gambling. These tend to enter fully into the fellowship and make a considerable contribution to it. They understand the programme and are enthusiastic about it. Some display an exceptional ability to inspire their group and to help new members. But unfortunately, while they enjoy their new life they are unable to hold on to it consistently. These problem gamblers show that the answer is not simply to attend more meetings.

Some come through in the end. They are usually the ones who, although given to bouts of gambling, never make the break with GA and eventually go on to make a settled and progressive recovery. However, there are others with a more complicated story to tell. One man enjoyed Gamblers Anonymous to the full for nearly two years. He expressed his delight in his new life at one meeting saying: 'I have been dead and now I am alive.' He made a success of his own recovery, inspired his group and took initiatives to establish others. Then, suddenly, he gambled again and since then has been unable to break absolutely with either gambling or Gamblers Anonymous.

Another man alternated, for months at a time, between gambling and Gamblers Anonymous. When he returned to gambling he hid the fact for as long as possible, but when he was forced to make the admission, he broke with the group again. Gamblers Anonymous deals patiently with them all. Men like this are always welcome because there is an abiding hope that perhaps this time they will 'get the message'. Yet as often seems to be the case hidden factors lie at the root of the problem and it is obviously best to seek the advice of a therapist or a counsellor.

Having looked at the GA problem cases it is now time to turn our attention to those members who establish the 'norm' for Gamblers Anonymous. These start their recovery from the first meeting or within a few weeks of becoming members, and continue to improve gradually with time. Their progress is seldom smooth, but they do manage to stop gambling. They usually don't return to it but go on to enjoy a progressive recovery.

There are variations in this pattern of course. In some cases the beginning of the recovery process is marked by a few 'slips' into gambling, although the member usually manages to recover his balance within a few weeks and gets back on to the recovery programme as soon as he can. Others, further from the 'norm', continue both to gamble and to attend meetings, often pretending that they have given it up. They can be considered to be close to the 'norm' because when they do break with gambling, they immediately get on with their recovery. Others who eventually come close to the 'norm' are those who, after apparently enjoying a period of recovery, leave GA and then, some time later, return and make a progressive recovery straight away.

It is my belief that those who represent or approximate to the 'norm' are those whose only major personal problem is gambling. They were caught by 'action' gambling and followed the way into problem gambling. They encounter difficulties on the way out but these are nothing that they can't deal with. Like the secretary of a local group of Gamblers Anonymous I referred to in chapter 3, once they are firmly on the road to recovery, they become their old, well-balanced selves again.

It is at this point, perhaps, that we should consider the idea that problem gambling is a sickness. As I suggested in chapter 6, members of GA are encouraged to accept the notion that being a compulsive gambler is a kind of illness. Similarly their wives, in Gam-Anon, are told that they could not help doing what they did because they were sick. But is this description of problem gambling as an illness justified? In my opinion it is – for two main reasons. In the first place to be carried away by gambling and to be obsessed with it in the way we described in chapter 3 involves the gambler in a loss of self-direction and self-control which is akin to the powerlessness felt by someone suffering from a progressive illness. Further, if this condition is to be corrected, help or 'treatment' from some quarter or other is necessary. For these reasons then, and because it forms an important part of a new member's self-recognition, I believe that Gamblers Anonymous is fully justified in describing compulsive gambling as an illness.

However even so, very early on in my experience I began to question the exact sense of the word 'illness' as used here. If these people were sick in the conventional sense, how were they capable of arresting, on the spot, something which had progressively increased its hold over them for twenty, thirty or maybe even forty years? And how, after about ten weeks, provided they were following the way to recovery, could they possibly be starting to accept responsibility for their past, present and future actions? When those suffering from a more recognizable illness could never be held completely responsible for their actions until after they had fully recovered? I came to the conclusion that they were sick, but not in the medical sense of the word.

Some people who come to Gamblers Anonymous are better described as dependent gamblers rather than as problem or compulsive ones. Dependence is a condition recognized by the medical profession as an illness and those who suffer from gambling dependence are, I understand, often unable to stop gambling at once and require professional help if they are to do so. However, the fact that some gamblers need alternative or additional help does not mean that Gamblers Anonymous is failing to deal with the problem or that it should add to the service it provides. It is 'nature's way' and should always be tried first because it has proved its efficacy time and time again. The challenge is to others, to academic psychologists, anthropologists and sociologists, to carry out research in these areas and to members of the caring professions, to explore ways of meeting this need. Some have risen to it; academics have studied problem gambling and members of the caring professions have given valuable help to problem gamblers of the most serious kind. Of these I must mention a number of pioneers with whom I have been fortunate enough to have been closely associated.

Dr Emanuel Moran has had problem gamblers as in- and out-patients for over 20 years. During the course of the time he has spent treating them, he found that, although they all have a gambling problem, they do not form a single homogenous group. Instead they can be divided into five sub-groups, only one of which he has identified as being composed of true compulsive or, as he prefers to call them, 'impulsive gamblers'. The excessive gambling of those in the other four sub-groups he has shown to be associated with another factor, condition or problem in the person's life – something which reinforces the argument I put forward earlier in this chapter about those Gamblers Anonymous members who do not conform to the norm.

Iain Brown, who has made a considerable contribution to the understanding of alcoholism and to the development of counselling services for alcoholics in Scotland, has also been associated with Gamblers Anonymous, of which he is an honorary member, for over 20 years. He has researched a number of the problem areas which have been discussed in this chapter and he has also provided much-needed counselling for problem gamblers.

The Sheffield group of Gamblers Anonymous was formed when Dr C. P. Seager asked for help in providing a programme of character development for four of his patients who had stopped gambling. Similarly the group in Exeter was formed at the suggestion of Dr Jim Orford and composed of his clients. Whilst Dr Mark Dickerson's research has provided valuable additions to our knowledge of problem gambling. Led by Dr Robert L. Custer, much has been done by therapists and researchers in the US, and other contributions have been made in Australia and some European countries. I could not hope to do justice to the work that these and others have done here but for those who want to know more, I have included a list of relevant titles in the Further Reading section at the back of this book.

However, compared with what is being done for those with alcohol or drug problems the facilities available for problem gamblers are still very limited, there are hardly any specialized treatment centres – and the information currently being supplied to the caring agencies is minimal. Why is this so? I think it is because problem drinkers and drug abusers are normally ultimately incapable of looking after themselves and start to become nuisances. They are then often picked up by the police and admitted to hospital for treatment. Their problem is an instantly recognizable one and the connection between it and their crimes is obvious.

In contrast, problem gamblers may be 'under the influence' 24 hours a day but this is not usually recognized because they stay on their feet. When they appear in court the connection between their gambling and their crimes is not obvious and is discovered only if reports are called for. So, the root cause of the gamblers' offence often goes completely undetected. In my innocence I thought that the very existence of Gamblers Anonymous and its progress through the UK would make it clear to everyone that compulsive or addictive gambling constitutes the significant problem that those of us who are involved with it know it to be. I expected that a thirst for information and a demand for facilities would follow at once. Unfortunately this did not prove to be the case. Nevertheless there was a reaction and one which I made the most of. Doctors, probation officers, social workers and others were among those who telephoned following the press conference for the UK launch of Gamblers Anonymous. They were interested in obtaining further help for their patients or clients and so, beginning in 1967, I convened a series of one-day conferences on compulsive gambling in London, Manchester and Glasgow – the first of their kind in the world as it turned out. From 1972 I organized and led bi-annual meetings of a Consultation on Compulsive Gambling which, five years later, became the Society for the Study of Gambling.

There are now other agencies in the UK, The National Council on Gambling, the Gordon House Association, (a hostel for single, homeless compulsive gamblers) and the Merseyside Council on Gambling Addictions, all of which are tackling the problem. Gamblers Anonymous has its own General Services Board to serve it and supplement its work. It produces teaching aids and organizes study days for the probation services and other similar organizations and members of Gamblers Anonymous address schools and various other organizations on frequent occasions.

There has been some response from the British Government. The Home Office Prison Department has encouraged prison governors to allow Gamblers Anonymous to form groups inside prisons. Gordon House now receives a deficit grant from the Home Office through the Stonham Housing Association. The Gamblers Anonymous General Services Board receives a small annual sum from the Voluntary Services Unit at the Home Office to help cover administrative costs. And the Merseyside Council on Gambling Addictions was set up with financial support from the local authority. However, this unfortunately is not enough. The reason for the lack of progress is simple. The case the relevant groups have put forward has failed to convince the people that matter because, as the Rothschild Royal Commission on Gambling reported in 1978, no one knows exactly how many people are affected. There is, in many ways, a kind of vicious circle – organizations involved in helping problem gamblers necessarily direct their efforts and limited resources mainly towards studying the psychology and emotional cost of compulsive gambling. But effective *official* action will not be taken to gather and disseminate information on this subject, to train statutory and voluntary workers, and to set up much-needed treatment facilities, unless the number of sufferers can be quantified and found to justify, to the people responsible, the expenditure involved.

That is a challenge to Gamblers Anonymous and to Gam-Anon. Problem gamblers who are still gamblers may not lie down to be counted, but will recovering problem gamblers stand up and be counted? This is Twelfth Step work, helping to carry the message to those who are still suffering. Anonymity would not be at risk. No names would be mentioned. There would be none of the involvement with outside issues or with other bodies which Gamblers

Anonymous so properly fears. It would simply be a matter of gathering and publishing numbers. Information about the nature and effects of the problem is published, why *not* information regarding the numbers involved?

It would not be difficult. A representative sample of willing groups would be sufficient. A trusted researcher could be found to set up and oversee the enquiry in association with the National Committee and one or two long-term members in each group could be given the responsibility of collecting the necessary statistics.

All of this will have to be done if an effective case is to be put before the authorities. Until we can supply these all-important figures, we shall have to accept that the training programmes for the medical profession and the social, probation and prison services, all of which have first-hand dealings with problem gamblers, will either neglect this subject or deal inadequately with it.

Even while we are working on that, though, three small tasks might be attempted. A university department might set up a research project to achieve the first. The purpose of this would be to locate the agencies up and down the country which already help problem gamblers and their families. If they were located and listed in this way they could escape the isolation they probably feel, by getting in touch with each other.

Second, we should be working towards providing the members of the caring agencies, many of whom are already helping problem drinkers and drug abusers, with the information, encouragement and facilities which will enable them to use their skills to help problem gamblers as well.

Finally, thought should be given to broadening and deepening the contacts between Gamblers Anonymous and Gam-Anon on the one hand, and the helping agencies on the other. Some therapists and counsellors recommend those who come to them for treatment to try Gamblers Anonymous as well. More could do the same. In the same way Gamblers Anonymous could encourage more interaction with the caring agencies. It is quite inward-looking in character and most who succeed there tend to believe, at least in their first years, that a compulsive gambler can be understood and helped nowhere else. This may be because, on the one hand, they felt so alone while they were gambling and, on the other, they now feel so understood and secure in the group. At any event, as a rule, members of Gamblers Anonymous have limited expectations where the caring agencies are concerned. They tend to see the role of professional workers as one of recognizing the problem and of referring those who suffer from it to Gamblers Anonymous or Gam-Anon. Their own role is to provide the information the professional workers require for this purpose. Perhaps if they could give this matter further thought, especially those members who are well along the road to recovery, this attitude might be modified. It would certainly help if individual members could start to suggest to those whose recovery appears to be blocked, that they should seek additional help elsewhere.

The Challenge

Sometimes a problem gambler needs additional and/or alternative help because, while Gamblers Anonymous works wonders for many, the recovery of others is blocked by other personal problems with which Gamblers Anonymous does not pretend to deal.

- Some, who need and want help to stop gambling, just do not settle in to Gamblers Anonymous, and need another environment.

- Some, however hard they try, fail to stay in Gamblers Anonymous ('in GA'), repeatedly returning to gambling.

- Some, who try desperately, fall back into gambling when other unresolved problems throw their lives into chaos.

- Some, who understand and welcome the programme and help others follow it, cannot successfully apply it to themselves.

- For some, gambling constitutes a mental illness for which they require help.

This is a challenge to the caring agencies. Some academics and some members of the caring agencies have made valuable contributions towards helping problem gamblers. However, because problem gamblers do not make nuisances of themselves and attract a great deal of attention the connection between their addiction and any crimes that they may commit is hidden. Because no one knows how many there are, their impact on society is underestimated with the result that the caring agencies are generally neither equipped nor trained to help them.

This, then, is a challenge for Gamblers Anonymous. It alone can count numbers. It alone can show the authorities that it would be worthwhile to join in the work to help those who still suffer, directly and indirectly, from problem gambling. This would be Twelfth Step work.

10
When wives or female partners are gamblers

What difference does it make if the wife and not the husband is the gambler? The difficulty about answering this question is that remarkably few women attend Gamblers Anonymous. So, while I have listened to hundreds of male problem gamblers and their wives or partners, I have met only a handful of women problem gamblers and even fewer of their husbands. It is possible, of course, that fewer women than men gamble and that when they do they are less likely than men to take it to extremes. What little research has been done into this area certainly seems to support this theory.

For a long time, I believed that as in the case of Alcoholics Anonymous, more women would gradually begin to attend meetings of Gamblers Anonymous. For many years, the membership of Alcoholics Anonymous had been predominantly male. Because excessive drinking was thought to be more degrading in a woman than in a man, many women alcoholics and their families had hidden their secret in shame. Then, when alcoholism was identified as an illness rather than as a moral offence, more women started to attend so that today, membership of Alcoholics Anonymous is split equally between men and women.

In fact this has not proved to be the case with Gamblers Anonymous. One woman attended the first British meeting in 1964. Since then few groups have had more than one female member at a time and never has there been, on average, one woman for each group in the UK. I believe that, in spite of all the changes that have taken place in recent years in society's attitudes to women and towards private and public morality, some women are still inhibited by that stigma from seeking help as problem gamblers. If any woman in thrall to gambling read this book, I hope they will be brave and determined enough to seek and find help.

None the less, I have met some women gamblers in Gamblers

Anonymous and the accounts they have given of their experiences have left me with a clear impression of the problems they face. Their way into problem gambling was the same as that followed by male gamblers. They were carried away by the 'action' and gradually their dream world and their impatience took their personality over so that eventually they too were gambling with their lives. What was different was the impact which gambling had on their lives.

In the first place and especially in the case of financially dependent wives, far fewer and far smaller debts were required to bring about a financial crisis. Worse still, the domestic crisis that accompanied it was almost always more severe, more painful and more critical.

In the second place, gambling mothers appeared to suffer more than gambling fathers. They have to know their children. The mother at the beginning of this book who was underfeeding her children in order to save the money she needed for the next bingo game had to know what she was doing to them. For her, that was not the worst of it. Women problem gamblers are also often led, by their gambling, to lie and steal. Her husband found money disappearing from his pockets. She had taken it but she laid the blame on her son. When accused the boy stuck up for her and did not give her away. So she had to live with the guilt of her betrayal too.

Gambling fathers on the other hand are only sometimes forced to recognize the harm they are doing to their children at the time it is happening. On those occasions they suffer terrible remorse and guilt, but most of the harm they do is indirect, caused by omission and neglect and as a result of their absence. Their distress comes later, when they are starting to recover. It is then that it comes home to them that, while they were gambling they did not know their children and they missed watching them grow up.

Thirdly, even when they are desperate to do so, some women hesitate to seek help because they are afraid that their gambling will be discovered. Towards the end of 1965, a woman actually telephoned the contact number for Gamblers Anonymous and spoke to me. She told me that she was in great difficulty as a result of gambling. It had started when her daughter, who had made a generous contribution to the housekeeping money, had married and left home. She had missed the money badly, especially as her husband had recently had to take a cut in wages. While out shopping, she had overheard some women talking about what they had won on the horses. She decided to place a bet herself but what started out as a 'one-off' event gradually began to take hold of her life. Soon she was hooked and losing. When she got too far behind to recoup her position by being careful, she used her husband's savings which he had put into her care to get out of debt. The money went on further bets as she tried to win her way out of trouble, becoming more and more desperate as time went on. Eventually it ran out and she was caught like a rat in a trap.

She was terrified that her husband would find out and she was sure she could never tell him. Afraid that if she came to a meeting of Gamblers Anonymous and revealed her secret, her husband would find out, she agreed to meet the only woman gambler at the time attending a London group at the entrance to a London Underground station some distance from her home. She did not keep the appointment. There was no more we could do.

About the same time I took a telephone call from another woman. She had been gambling for some time and was well behind with household and other bills. To get money to gamble she had resorted to prostitution. Now things were beginning to come to a head and she did not know where to turn. She was too frightened even to give her first name or telephone number.

She insisted that she could not confide in her husband. She knew him she said and she was sure that, with the gambling, the debts and the prostitution she had gone far, far beyond anything he could understand, let alone accept and forgive. Again there was little we could do to help.

Even when the husband or partner of a gambler becomes aware of his wife's problem, he is less likely than the wife of a gambling husband to help find the way to recovery and to accompany her along it. Generally, as the examples of gambling husbands in previous chapters have shown, a gambler's wife quickly spots that he has a problem and then tries to find out what it is. Once it has been identified, she concentrates on helping him to resolve it. She is also willing to admit that she too has problems and is prepared to share in his recovery. Unfortunately however, this pattern, which is the norm for the Gamblers Anonymous/Gam-Anon relationship, does not apply in cases where the wife is the gambler. The nearest one husband got to admitting that there might be a problem was when he asked his wife why she never seemed to get her hair done or buy a new dress. She took it as a criticism of her appearance and things did not come to a head until a long time after.

Another woman I visited needed and wanted her husband's help. He earned good money and gave her a fair proportion of it. She had two part time jobs but both did her more harm than good. She sold sheets, towels and blankets on commission and also ran a mail order catalogue. Most of the proceeds, together with much of the housekeeping money, went into gambling machines, and her debts were soon overwhelming her. She tried to tell her husband, but he sensed that he was going to hear about a problem which would complicate his life, and he took up his cap claiming that he had to see a friend about some business and went out.

A woman wrote to me about her problem in the early years of Gamblers Anonymous when correspondence still came to my office. She was deeply enmeshed in gambling and had debts she could not pay. I replied immediately, sending the original letter to the appropriate group secretary. I advised her to tell her husband everything as she was too far from any group to attend. She replied saying that she had been unable to do this directly and had told her story as though it concerned someone else. He had reacted by saying that if it had been her she would have been beaten and thrown out of the house.

Husbands can often make recovery more difficult for women who attend Gamblers Anonymous. One woman member of a group of Gamblers Anonymous had debts which were, in comparison with those of other members, very small. She owed accounts to several shops. She was in a state of crisis because she could not pay them. Following the advice of the group, she told her husband. He went to his mother, told her the whole story, gave her the money and asked her to pay the bills. Soon everyone knew that this woman owed hundreds of pounds to every shopkeeper in the district. She stopped attending the meetings but did she recover? I doubt it, her husband's misguided actions may well have prevented her from ever holding her head up again.

Another woman attending a London meeting said that she was finding recovery difficult because she was still handling the housekeeping money. The male members of the group were able to sympathize with her because they knew how much the fact that their wives looked after the money was helping them. For them carrying money was the equivalent of a drug addict carrying heroin. They suggested that she should ask her husband to take control. She told him that she was still in danger of gambling the money she earned, and the money he and their daughter gave her, but he refused to help her. His attitude was that she was the woman of the family so it was her duty to deal with these things.

Perhaps it is more likely that husbands will just walk out and leave their wives to their fate. This leaves women in great danger, but free to go to Gamblers Anonymous. One woman who did this, after being left by a second husband, took the step just in time – she had been on the point of selling her car and her maisonette for gambling money.

The men who do become aware of their wives' problems and encourage them to go to Gamblers Anonymous tend to stay in the background, perhaps taking an interest in their wife's recovery and attending open meetings and social occasions. Some may attend Gam-Anon meetings, at least for a while, but they are few and far between. Traditional conceptions and attitudes make it hard for a man to sit with women who have suffered at the hands of their men and to admit that he has suffered in the same way at the hands of a woman, particularly if he is the only man.

When I think of the future of the couples to whom I have referred, I can see little but division, separation and divorce. This is no substitute for a true cure. In such cases, the offender is invariably left with feelings of shame and remorse and a sense of grievance for not having been understood while the offended suffers wounded pride, anger and a sense of having been betrayed. The rest of their lives are poisoned with bitter memories of the past. We shall consider this aspect of recovery in the next chapter.

Women gamblers – their particular problems

Few women attend Gamblers Anonymous, possibly, though not certainly, because fewer women become problem gamblers.

Those who do attend have special problems, not with gambling, but because of society's attitudes towards women. A 'special' stigma attaches to women who gamble to excess. Gambling mothers suffer more than gambling fathers. The mother usually spends more time with the children and is therefore continually being reminded of the fact that she is neglecting them and harming them. In contrast, most gambling fathers are hardly aware of their children as they grow up.

Financially dependent wives are often too frightened to seek help in case their husbands are informed of the extent of their gambling and of their debts.

While wives generally support and help gambling husbands in their recovery, husbands are less likely to do the same for gambling wives. Some husbands, when finally faced with their wife's gambling, simply leave home.

While some husbands take an interest in their wives' recovery only a few attend Gam-Anon. Most would find it difficult to sit with women who had suffered at the hands of their husbands and admit that they had suffered in a similar way at the hands of their wives.

11

The His and Hers of recovery

What I have written in the previous chapter has led me to consider the implications of a change which has taken place in Gam-Anon. From 1964 onwards it was almost the rule that for every man in Gamblers Anonymous there was a woman in Gam-Anon. More recently, things have changed, and today some Gamblers Anonymous groups operate without Gam-Anon. In other cases only a small proportion of Gamblers Anonymous members are accompanied by their partners. This can be explained in part by the fact that today, many members are younger than their predecessors were and are often still single. However, in the case of those who are married, the wife now often makes a deliberate choice not to come.

This development no doubt relates to the social and economic changes which, in the past few decades, have affected the position of women in the home and in society. Life for the earliest members of Gam-Anon, compared with its nature now for the partners of those who come to Gamblers Anonymous, was a very different affair.

For a number of years from 1964, the average age of Gam-Anon members must have been at least forty. Most grew up, and many of them married, either before or during the Second World War. At that time it was common for women to give up work on marriage and in some occupations it was compulsory. Even when married women continued to work, their wages were usually far less than those of men. As well as this the social security system had been in operation only sixteen years when Gam-Anon came to the United Kingdom in 1964. The wives of the younger men who now come to Gamblers Anonymous were born into a world to which the first members of Gam-Anon had to adapt.

The late-twentieth-century gambler's wife is a different person because she is living in a different world. Her improved status enables her to feel stronger and more independent than her mother and grandmother did at her age. If she has a job and does not have a family she can refuse to put up with a partner who persistently causes her too much pain. She can leave him or tell him to go. If she has older children and a job, though it will be more difficult, life can be managed and organized in a way that would be impossible if she was still living with her gambling husband. Even if she is a housewife with young children she still has a choice. To live on one parent benefit is hard but arguably better than living with a compulsive gambler.

Being in a position to feel stronger and more independent gives her two advantages over the original members of Gam-Anon. In the first place it enables her to take the stand we described in chapter 5 more effectively and so help her husband to reach rock bottom more quickly. Secondly, instead of just pleading or advising, she can issue ultimatums which are much more likely to concentrate the gambler's mind. Those who do not attend Gam-Anon tend to see gambling as their husband's problem and believe that he should sort it out for himself. If he cannot or will not do so, he knows that the relationship may end.

Such gambling husbands have two advantages over some of the gambling wives we met in the previous chapter. They are more likely to be encouraged to attend Gamblers Anonymous and they usually have the means to undertake for themselves the responsibility of budgeting and clearing their debts. However, recovery will not be complete if it is not shared. Indeed, its progress will be impeded for both the gambler and his or her partner if partners unsympathetically dissociate themselves from it. Take the case of the man I mentioned in chapter 4 who made his prison sentence part of his recovery programme because he had attended Gamblers Anonymous before his trial for embezzlement.

I went to see his wife while he was waiting to come before the magistrate. Her patience had obviously been tested to breaking point long before and she was sceptical when I said he was going to Gamblers Anonymous. She clearly thought he had deceived me and was hoping to deceive Gamblers Anonymous and the Court too. They had been married for about thirty years and she was now earning her own living and had created her own independent life. Though he came and went, she had made sure she was no longer able to be hurt by anything he did. I don't think that really changed when he came home from prison although he did not return to gambling, found new employment, prospered and blossomed as a person. Who could blame her? Who could expect more, remembering the past? Yet I could see that the distance she kept from him while living as his wife in the same house, was affecting them both adversely.

Though she could not be blamed, her inability to try to understand, to risk trying to trust him, made his recovery more difficult. She was bound by memories of his previous behaviour and could not let go. Ultimately, the situation was of his own making and he would have to deal with it himself if he was to make a full recovery. Unfortunately it was something which he was unable to handle and a few years later he went back to gambling. In this case it was the wife's determination not to be hurt again which dealt the final blow. The defences she erected against him sealed within her all her past hurt which festered like an unhealed wound and in this way she prevented herself from making the recovery she needed. At the same time she made it impossible for her husband to get away from his guilt. He needed an opportunity to make up for all that he had done to her in the past by treating her properly in the present and the future but because of her behaviour, this way was effectively closed to him.

The same thing happened to another couple I knew. The wife attended Gam-Anon but did not become committed to it. Her husband struggled on and fought to stay away from gambling for a while but he did not enjoy a recovery in the proper sense of the word. When I asked him how things were going one evening he told me that his wife just couldn't let go of the past. Soon after this, he stopped attending.

Even if she does not attend Gam-Anon, a gambler's wife needs to make her own recovery. The suffering of the Gam-Anon wife today may be shorter but it is still extremely intense. She may be strong and independent but people do not enter marriage relying on their defences. They enter it to become involved with each other and that makes them vulnerable, each before the other. Of course, such a wife may not know that she has a recovery to make. There is nothing new about this attitude either. From the early days wives often initially attended Gam-Anon meetings as part of their strategy for getting their husbands to go to Gamblers Anonymous. However, the longer they stayed the more they became aware of their need to deal with their own problems.

Just after Gam-Anon came to the UK, a young woman called to ask for help for her husband. He had just gone to prison for crimes committed in order to fund his gambling. She wanted someone to go to the prison and counsel him. This was arranged but when asked if she needed any help herself she rejected the idea at once. *She* was not a gambler. Her voice was clear and confident. She had no shadow of doubt. Fortunately the network was strong and she was persuaded that she as well as her husband needed the help that was being offered. Along with many others who, at their first meeting, think that only their husbands need help, she was grateful for the efforts which were made to convince her that she too needed to make a recovery.

Sometimes, after years of shared recovery and of rebuilding a marriage, one or both partners realize that it is still not working. In such cases they usually find that all the work they have put in to understanding and forgiving each other pays dividends. It helps them to manage separation or divorce in a much more constructive way. Those who divorce gambling partners, without the reconciliation that this kind of recovery brings, are left with a life still plagued by unresolved bitterness, mistrust, a need for revenge and all the other attitudes and emotions which blight relationships and distort personalities. Time may superficially heal the wounds but the scars will remain.

In the first years, life in the close-knit fellowships of Gamblers Anonymous and Gam-Anon was wonderful, husbands and wives (or partners) were sharing their recovered lives with other couples. Those of us who experienced it often regret the change that has taken place. In those days, when the meeting was over, people stayed in happy clusters in the courtyard or street outside, in a cafe or public house, sharing the joys of their new life. I have never known company like it. I specifically remember the first anniversary party, held on 10 July 1965, in an upstairs room of the Black Horse public house in London. No one was more than a year out of misery and everyone knew they were happier now than they had ever been. There was a great sense of belonging and a feeling of exhileration which it is impossible to describe.

Of course there were problems too. Some men who were accustomed to the idea that they should be the dominant partner in their marriages tended to resent Gam-Anon and to discourage or prevent their wives from attending. Others, when they found that it was encouraging their partners to have high expectations of them and demand evidence of change, began to look upon it as a dirty tricks department which was bent on teaching previously compliant wives to be awkward. Fortunately, however, most members recognized that this was all part of the co-operation and support their wives were giving them.

New members were advised to bring their wives along. 'They get to understand you'. Experienced members were inclined to try to persuade a wife to stay with a new member 'to give him a chance' if she had said she had decided to leave him. If his wife had already left him, the new member was consoled that, if he proved himself, she might come back. Recovering your life means recovering your relationships as we shall see in chapter 13 when we consider the recovery of problem gamblers who have lost their families.

In chapter 14 we will deal with the third stage of recovery in which members of both Gamblers Anonymous and Gam-Anon concentrate on progressive personality and character development. This can be achieved only in the context of relationships which are being healed and renewed or, after separation or divorce, freshly created. Those who attempt that stage, whether as single people or as partners, often set themselves goals which they might never have attempted had not gambling intervened to force them to examine their lives.

They leave many of us behind in this endeavour. In life we are generally accustomed to putting up with dissatisfying or distant relationships and often we don't realize what we are missing. I hope that what I have said will encourage the partners of gamblers to recognize that there is a better life on offer, and to go out and seize it with both hands.

12

Child gamblers

Only in recent years has child problem gambling become a matter of public concern. However, it is not a recent development. Indeed, from the early years the proportion of members of Gamblers Anonymous who have traced the onset of their problems (as well as of their gambling) to their childhood has consistently stood at more than 70 per cent. One man recalled one Saturday morning when his mother sent him to do some shopping in town. On the way to the shops he saw some children throwing pennies against the wall and joined in the game. As a result, he lost the money his mother had given him so he stole mint from some allotments and sold it in penny bundles from house to house in order to make up what he had lost. When he had collected enough money he started on his way to the shops again, but was again distracted by another 'game' and lost every penny that he had collected. Late at night, driven by exhaustion, he went home to his punishment. Although this is the story of a young boy, it nevertheless represents a classic example of the problem gambler. The 'grip' of gambling, the impatience, the dream world, the stealing, the total lack of concern for others, all of these are symptoms which we have come across before. Even so, this individual's progress into problem gambling was slow because opportunities for 'action' gambling in those days were relatively few and far between.

Today things are different. Opportunities for 'action' gambling abound for children and young people and in recent years there has been a small flood of this group to Gamblers Anonymous – they now account for about one in four of all new members. They are usually involved with prize machines, sophisticated versions of the 'one-armed bandit' or 'fruit machines' which provide the experience of casino gaming, 'action' gambling at its most intense. Most towns have amusement centres and since there are no legal age limits on entry, it is easy for children to fall victim to them. When they do, their progress into problem gambling is very rapid indeed.

The development of problem gambling in these children usually follows a general pattern. They start to get interested in the machines at the age of eight or nine. By the time they've reached 11 they've already become seriously involved in playing the machines and their character is beginning to undergo a change. At 13 they are probably stealing from their parents and friends to get money for gambling so that by the time they are 16 they have probably already been in trouble with the police.

I could cite a number of cases of child gamblers here but there is not really any need. We know how gambling affects the individual and children suffer in much the same way as adults. What does need to be dealt with in some detail is the way in which relationships within the family are affected by a child gambler.

The child's parents notice changes in behaviour early on but often put them down to adolescence. However when they hear from the school that their child's work has seriously deteriorated, that he* has become aggressive and is involved in playground fights, they start to worry. He starts to lose weight because he is using his lunch money to play the machines and his health suffers. Things begin to disappear from his room and from the house. He becomes sullen, withdrawn, uncommunicative – a stranger in their house. They know now that he has a problem but they have no idea what it is. Perhaps it's drugs, but the evidence is against that. When they ask him what is wrong he pretends that everything is fine and asks them what they are worrying about. They decide to resort to corporal punishment but it fails leaving them humiliated and confused. They begin to feel undermined and to lose confidence in themselves and their ability to bring up their own children. They ask themselves where they went wrong and blame each other for something which neither of them can control.

Often the truth comes home to them in a crisis, usually when a policeman knocks at the door. At this point the shock and fright will probably induce a confession from the child. His parents won't know how to react. They are relieved to discover what is wrong but angry and ashamed their child could have done this to them and they fear for the future. However, when they see how much their child is suffering their love for him will usually sweep all that away.

It is a very distressing time for other children in the family too. They feel involved in some way in his 'crime' and tainted by it. They cannot understand how he could have got involved in such a stupid activity. Their relationship with him breaks down.

A court case often brings matters to a head. The child has fallen on to a 'ledge' which could, if the situation is handled properly, be rock bottom for him (see chapter 4 and page 50). At this time his parents should try to introduce him to Gamblers Anonymous, with the minimum of fuss, adopting a warm but restrained supporting role. This move does not always succeed. Although the child might desperately want to break with gambling and be reconciled to his family, he probably doesn't know how to go about it. He feels alone and frightened and suffers guilt and shame. He has lost his self-respect and mustn't on any account lose face. If a man can't handle this situation, how can we expect a child to? Gambling is his escape from himself as well as his addiction.

Parents, who would usually be drawn together by trouble, often find themselves being pulled apart at this time. Child gamblers know exactly when to put pressure on one or the other of them or on both and they may find themselves being played off one against the other, to the child's advantage. In this way marriages are put at risk, one parent wants the child to go, the other opposes this, terrified at the prospect of leaving the child alone and at the mercy of his own gambling problem. When they cannot agree, the situation usually deteriorates and they may even separate.

If this happens then the parent who wanted to continue caring for the child will have to endure the problem on his or her own. One woman I met who had separated from her husband because of his intolerance towards their gambling son, had to keep her possessions under lock and key to stop the child gambling them away. Another sat with her son, night in, night out, watching his every movement. He was a chain-smoker, smoking her cigarettes. At his slightest motion she gave him another, it was as though he was sucking the life blood from her. Both of these women were totally lost and bewildered and had no hope that things would get better or that they could change them.

Although the chain-smoking young gambler above may appear passive, he sometimes displayed his pent-up frustration by punching doors in his home – and the mother of another young gambler was able to tell his mother that her own son had behaved in exactly the same way.

Now that more publicity is being given to the problem of child gambling, parents may be on the look-out for it. If they spot, and catch it in its very early stages, which is not easy to do, they may be able to nip it in the bud. There is scant knowledge from past experience to go on, but some parents, by exercising close and loving supervision, have kept their children away from the machines and organized their activities in other directions, thus weaning their children away from gambling before an obsession develops.

If it is already too late, parents must develop a strategy for containing the situation. Because they will need each other's support they should also work on their own relationship. They should try to introduce and preserve quiet areas in their family life for themselves and their other children. When dealing with the problem child, self-control is essential. You might be tempted to shout at the child, reproaching, scolding and cajoling him. This is useless. If your questions are met with lies or absolute resistance, any interrogation should cease. If a child apparently has to gamble, lie and steal, there is no point in nagging – this will only harm the relationship you have with them.

What has to be accepted is that, although the child is still a child, the problem is his and dealing with it is, therefore, his responsibility. The debts and difficulties resulting from his gambling should be seen as his responsibility too. However, if your child is a problem gambler you must try to provide him with firm, supportive love at all times. A place must be kept for him in the family and you should try to draw him in to a shared activity since, as with adult problem gamblers, he will not have complete control over his life. It will seem an unending and thankless task and you will need help in tackling it. Talk to Gam-Anon. In the UK contact Parents of Young Gamblers. They will be able to provide you with the support you need.

Parents resist sending their children away from home, however, if they leave of their accord, *when they are in their late teens*, parents experience relief as well as pain and anxiety. They can, as a result, relax and give time and attention to their other children. They still worry, of course, and fear that any day they will have bad news. Even so, they realize that while their child is still gambling he must not return. They know that they could not help, and that it would be impossible for them or their other children to cope if all the problems started again.

There is hope. There are signs that today's child problem gamblers are being accelerated through and out of the experience as well as into it. Some who were brought unsuccessfully to Gamblers Anonymous as children are now returning of their own accord a few years later. Others who did not attend Gamblers Anonymous during their childhood but whose parents have been helped by Parents of Young Gamblers in the past are now beginning to give up gambling as they pass from their teens.

Although to actually stop gambling is a big step, it is only the first in the battle against the problem. Reorientation, a move away from the gambling frame of mind and way of life, must also occur if the child is to make a full recovery. Those who attend Gamblers Anonymous will be shown the necessity of this and will be encouraged to see that there must be an absolute change, a new direction, and no looking back. They will be encouraged to say sorry and mean it, to meet new people and to share their feelings with them. They will be shown a way which will teach them the value of creating a new life, a new mind and a new outlook. It will not be an easy one to follow but with the trust and acceptance of their close family and friends there is no reason why they should not succeed.

*The child in this chapter is referred to as 'he' as experience has shown that relatively few girls are child gamblers.

Child gamblers – the problem and an approach to dealing with it

Child gambling is not new. Most adult problem gamblers can trace the beginning of their gambling and the onset of their problems back to their childhood.

Fruit-machines have been responsible for accelerating problem gambling in child gamblers, introducing them to 'action' gambling at an early stage. Typically, they start to 'play' at 8 or 9, are 'hooked' by 11 and start to steal by 13 so that by 16 the policeman is at the door.

The child's personality begins to change. He becomes withdrawn, uncommunicative, sullen, a stranger in the house. His parents are puzzled at first and put his behaviour down to adolescence. When things do not improve however, they become worried and then distraught.

If the problem is recognized early enough it may be arrested by exercising close and loving supervision and encouraging the child to take part in other activities. However, the truth usually comes home in a crisis when the police are at the front door.

Child gamblers – the problem and an approach to dealing with it (cont.)

A child gambler affects everyone in the family. He will play parents off against each other, so that they blame their partner and may even separate as a result.

They are tempted to thrash him, but if they do, they end up feeling humiliated and even more angry.

Outside the home, brothers and sisters are embarrassed. Inside, they quarrel bitterly with the gambler when he takes their possessions and sells them to raise money he needs to continue to 'play'.

Once the problem is discovered parents should:

● Get in touch with Gamblers Anonymous or Parents of Young Gamblers.

● Keep a quiet area of family for themselves and their other children.

● Refrain from useless nagging – avoid asking the gambler child pressing questions if they know that they will only get lies in return.

● Lay the responsibility for the gambling and its consequences on the child himself or herself.

● Make sure the child is aware that there is support and love available to him/her, get the child involved as often as possible in family activities.

The gambling may go on for many years or it may cease by the time the child reaches adulthood.

13

A ledge too far

What about those problem gamblers who, missing all the ledges and potential rock bottoms, fall into solitary homelessness? From 1964 to 1971 I met many of them, simply because the office of the Churches' Council on Gambling provided headquarters for Gamblers Anonymous. Drawn by that name they came to look over the edge of the gutter hoping that someone would haul them out of it.

The effort transformed them. When you see them in the street, hanging onto a ragged existence, sleeping rough, containing themselves in a guarded and self-conscious anonymity – they walk with eyes averted in crowded streets and look like sad shells which the human occupants have departed.

All this changed when they came to talk to us, because in talking they became people again. Some, sad little people – inadequately equipped for life, stirred my deepest sympathy. Most were interesting and lively. I warmed to them all.

They set me a problem. All had started life *somewhere*. Some had enjoyed both a parental and a marital home. How was it then that those who were succeeding in Gamblers' Anonymous had heeded the warning signs in time and sought help while they still had a home and a family, while others chose to ignore all the red lights?

The secret, in most cases, I believe, is that those who make the final fall have no one left who they can cling to, no one who is still holding on to them. One recovering gambler said in a letter that had it not been for his wife he would have ended up sleeping rough in cardboard city. It is difficult to make a successful rock bottom of a lonely furnished room. A room cannot respond to the efforts you are making. As one GA member said, shortly before he left his group, 'I go back to that room and ask myself: "What am I achieving here?" '

A partner can feel and respond and will make your efforts seem worth while. Having someone around aids recovery. Having someone insisting on staying around can secure a vital ledge from which you can make your recovery so that you never make that final fall. But for those who have no supportive relatives, no encouraging friends, the struggle to climb out of the pit is one which is not always successful. It is not enough to offer a helping hand – they need the guarantee of a sympathetic and supportive environment. The extreme difficulty this type of problem gambler faces, when attempting to make a recovery, was brought home to me by various men who stayed in touch with me – whether or not they were attending Gamblers Anonymous. I only have space to mention two at any length (I have changed their names to ensure their anonymity).

I knew Tommy over a perod of about six years. He formed the habit of dropping into my office for a chat – and while he was with me he became a great deal of what he aspired to be. I tended to forget his other life, away from my office, but it was thrown into sharp relief for me one Friday.

Tommy came to visit me in the late afternoon and we talked while I cleared up for the weekend and as we walked to my underground station. As we parted company I said, without thinking: 'Have a good weekend'. Friends said it to each other all the time. It was a cliché I immediately regretted. His face changed as he strode on. It closed in and became expressionless. His shoulders hunched and his head bowed forward as if he was walking into a storm. It was not a reaction to what I had said. He was facing his weekend, with nowhere to go and nowhere to sleep.

He had great moments. Just out of prison, a debt to society paid, happily in Gamblers Anonymous for the time being, with a bed to sleep in but not yet in employment, he came to see me. I sent him by train to see a gambler in the Midlands who had written for help. He was a persuasive emissary. He came back triumphant and the man to whom he went is in Gamblers Anonymous to this day.

David came into my life just before the Westminster office of the Churches' Council on Gambling closed. The work was moved to my house in Berkshire so we relied a good deal on correspondence. He had a nice sense of humour – writing to me from prison: 'Both your letters arrived safe and sound and censorised'. In just over seven years he sent 62 postcards and 35 letters. I wrote to him at five prisons and five hostels.

There are essential imbalances in such friendships and our correspondence reveals them. Most of the cards came when he had no address and was simply keeping in touch. Although he always knew where I was, I could never be sure of his whereabouts. He was, however, keen that I should write to him as a friend and not purely as someone to be supported and given encouragement. He wrote:

> *I received your letter on Sunday last and it was a pleasure to hear from you again. Try to remember next time you write to this geezer, or see him, that your intended recipient would, also, always like to know how the sender is keeping himself.*

The inward situation of a homeless person has possibly never been described better than by David. In his first letter to me, on a Post Office Letter Card, giving his address as the Trafalgar Square Post Office, he wrote:

> *My circumstances have not altered beneficially since I last saw you at Abbey House (my late office). To put it briefly, my mental computer and my natural engine are still reversing backwards. The reason why I've kept away from the (Gamblers Anonymous) meetings is because, at the present time, I'd be very similar to a person who attended an alcoholics meeting and carried with him a bottle of Scotch for his refreshment.*

Some years later when he was in Gordon House (described in detail later in this chapter), where I think he had his best time, he wrote:

> *My problems are my private possessions and the motivations are very obscure, even to me, but nobody in this house, or part of this house, has any extending influence on those problems whatsoever.*

For Tommy and David the importance of the last ledge on the way down and the first ledge on the way up always loomed large. Each ledge is a room somewhere. I met Tommy at his first Gamblers Anonymous meeting when he was on the last ledge down. His girl-friend had left him. He had a room, debts and many problems. In spite of Gamblers Anonymous that ledge was not a rock bottom for him. On one or two occasions while I knew him he managed to get a brief, tenuous hold on the first ledge up but this was only ever temporary. When I last saw him, he just wanted money and was unable to talk to me reasonably. He no longer felt he 'belonged' anywhere and had given up trying to conform or fit in. My contact with David ended with his last postcard which said simply: 'Christian Barnard (pioneer of heart transplants) cannot control ALL flutters.'

Those who come to this pass are constantly prey to dark and destructive thoughts – they know they have done harm, destroyed relationships and lost opportunities, they know that nothing can be repaid, repaired or recovered – these feelings form an indigestible lump within them and give rise to a smouldering and impotent anger. This, combined with their present degradation, drives them into a defensive isolation. They feel rejected and compensate by rejecting the rest of the human race. By despising society, its members and institutions, they try to bury their own self-contempt, self-loathing and self-condemnation. There were those who did manage to work their way up the ledges to recovery, but only a very few of the homeless men who attended Gamblers Anonymous succeeded in rehabilitating themselves.

A special hostel for single, homeless compulsive gamblers seemed to me a necessity if they were to have a chance to recover successfully. I saw it as providing them with a firm foothold and an encouraging environment for their recovery, a way back into society. I envisaged a place in central London, with easy access for referrals from Gamblers Anonymous and for self-referral from the street.

It has not yet been possible to establish a facility on exactly these lines – but as a result of my own work and that of many others (see Special Note at the end of this chapter) Gordon House was opened in 1971, in Beckenham, Kent. It is a hostel for single, homeless compulsive gamblers who are also ex-offenders, and Home Office funds were provided for it.

The residents come from a variety of backgrounds. Some were once public school boys but at least half have been in care as children, spending much of their time in institutions. This is quite understandable. When people in these circumstances take the wrong turning they do not have the same strong personal ties which others with families are likely to have developed. They are, therefore, more likely not to stay on the ledges from which they could start their recovery. Many of the residents have personal problems besides gambling and all have additional problems which developed during the course of their careers as gamblers and offenders. They are often emotionally insecure and have low tolerance levels. Their social skills and powers of communication are diminished but they hang on with determination to a sense of human dignity, a ragged remnant of personal pride. If they think they are being slighted, their reaction is usually swift, unpredictable and uncontrolled.

As a result life at Gordon House is fairly tropical. There are sudden squalls and violent storms but there are also periods of calm and sunshine. In the sunny spells, which can last for several months, the residents make progress and enjoy a quality of life they could not yet individually create and sustain.

However, months of effort may be destroyed in a moment. One man, when he arrived, had lost almost all ability to communicate. He slowly improved to the point where he could take up employment in a cafe in the local park. Then one night there was a break-in. The manager, although he had no evidence and made no accusation, made it clear that he suspected our resident. The resident, aware of being suspected, was at once under stress and could not frame a reply. He walked out in silent anger and worked it off by breaking into the cafe that night, perpetrating damage and stealing a few things. Then he ran and spent two weeks in petty crime, gambling and sleeping rough. The Warden had news of him when he was arrested several counties away.

Such experiences are not uncommon and yet visitors are usually instantly aware of the successes that Gordon House does achieve in the quality of its daily life. This was emphasized by the reaction of one female member of a television crew who came to film a short documentary at Gordon House. The crew had lunch with residents, staff and members of the management committee. Afterwards she said, 'That was real conversation', contrasting it with the superficial chit-chat that passes for conversation at many social gatherings. I think she was also surprised that the conversation was led and directed by the residents.

Real conversation goes on all the time at Gordon House. The weekly house meeting gives residents a chance to talk about a whole range of issues from a discussion of their own and each other's progress through to matters concerning the running of the house, all of which is of great therapeutic value. In addition, the staff are always ready to provide counselling in an emergency and each resident has the opportunity to discuss their progress, the efforts they are making and the difficulties they are facing, at a private weekly session.

On occasions, some residents have found it helpful to attend Gamblers Anonymous. But it does not always work – those who are struggling to keep their feet on a hostel floor do not easily relate to householders who are regaining self-respect as husbands and fathers. It is sad that the recovery programme is, as a result, not readily available to them to provide a structure for their struggle. They after all have to work doubly hard on their recovery. Seldom is there a family to which they can return, rarely are there any wounded but still existing relationships to be healed. In their wake, they have left an army of people whom they have harmed and to whom they are in debt, but there is no way that they can meet them and make amends. They are undermined by guilt but they are not able to get relief by going back and seeking forgiveness. Instead they have to move forward, coming to a new way of thinking and living through the fashioning of new relationships and the grasping of new opportunities. The most is demanded, in the process of recovery, from those with the fewest and most damaged resources.

Since it does not take much to upset the delicate balance which exists at Gordon House, only those who can convince the staff and the other residents that they really intend to change are accepted. The house draws strength from its successes. At first these were counted in the weeks that money was available to pay the rent, in days during which self-control and reasonable communication were maintained. Greater success was measured by weeks without a gamble and months rather than weeks between offences and periods of imprisonment.

These successes have been added to in the years that followed the opening of Gordon House. By arrangement with housing associations, flats are now provided for residents who are ready to move to a place of their own. And one of the other 'success stories' of Gordon House was present when we opened the enlarged and improved premises in December, 1987 – he was an *ex*-resident who had been in and out of the house twice before he was successful the third time. He was now married, with a family and a good job – he had not gambled for *ten* years.

Special Note

I must at least mention the names of a few people whose efforts were essential in creating Gordon House. Without Major James Breckenbridge of the Bridgehead Housing Association and the Reverend J.B. Harrison of the Church of England Council for Social Aid we would never have got off the ground. There are others who have sustained the development of Gordon House and these include the Stonham Housing Association, of which the Gordon House Association is now an agency. The staff and managers of the house have, of course, made an immeasurable contribution. But the history of the house should perhaps be written in terms of its residents – they have, above all, taught us just what help single, homeless compulsive gamblers need.

14

Recovery – a continuous process

So far we have looked at the recovery of problem or compulsive gamblers in three stages. Stage 1 was the subject of chapter 6 and stage 2 the subject of chapter 8. At the close of chapter 6, however, it was pointed out that the order in which the stages occur is not chronological. There is only one experience and progress is *into* its various aspects and not *through* them. The experience is described in this way to help non-gamblers like me who are trying to understand what is going on. The first stage concerned re-orientation, and the second covered the direction, progress and achievement of the recovery. The third is concerned with reflection on the experience of recovery, on its deeper implications and further progress in personal development. We are now going to deal with that stage.

To do this we have to look in some detail at the Gamblers Anonymous Recovery Programme. Members of Gam-Anon who help each other to deal with their own problems use an almost identical programme. This was adapted, with some freedom, from the one used by Alcoholics Anonymous and Al-Anon. In one form or another it will be familiar to members of many other self- or mutual-help groups. The programme reads as follows:

When a compulsive gambler applies the 12-step recovery programme in his life, his disintegration stops and his unification begins. These steps are basically spiritual in their concept and their practice can be highly rewarding. These are the steps which are suggested as a programme of recovery.

Gamblers Anonymous 12-step recovery programme

1 We admitted we were powerless over gambling – that our lives had become unmanageable.

2 Came to believe that a Power greater than ourselves could restore us to a normal way of thinking and living.

3 Made a decision to turn our will and our lives over to the care of this Power of our own understanding.

4 Made a searching and fearless moral and financial inventory of ourselves.

5 Admitted to ourselves and to another human being the exact nature of our wrongs.

6 Were entirely ready to have these defects of character removed.

7 Humbly ask God (of our understanding) to remove our shortcomings.

8 Made a list of all persons we have harmed and became willing to make amends to them all.

9 Made direct amends to such people wherever possible, except when to do so would injure them or others.

10 Continued to take personal inventory and when we were wrong, promptly admitted it.

11 Sought through prayer and meditation to improve our conscious contact with God as we understand Him, praying only for knowledge of His will for us and the power to carry that out.

12 Having made an effort to practise these principles in all our affairs, we tried to carry this message to other compulsive gamblers.

It is easy to understand why the word spiritual is applied to the programme by both Gamblers Anonymous and Gam-Anon. It certainly makes great demands on those members of both fellowships who seriously attempt to follow it – they have seen themselves, over the years, turn into the sort of people they dislike.

Members of Gam-Anon, I believe, generally enter upon this process sooner and more naturally than their partners in Gamblers Anonymous. During the course of their first few meetings they tend to purge their inner selves pretty violently. When that is done, when they are able to come out of themselves they can look at themselves clearly and begin to make a positive personal recovery.

The process of coming out of himself is I believe much harder for the gambler. As we saw in chapter 2, this wonderful gambling world has become for him a vortex, whirling him round and bearing him down relentlessly to the gutter, to prison or to suicide. At that point his obsession with gambling is at its deepest. Deviousness and deception have become second nature, and he shrinks right within himself, losing all contact with people and with life. Consequently, the time he will need in stage 2 to work his way out of that will be far greater although when he finally does emerge, he too will see himself more clearly as he is and can then set out on stage 3.

I realized very early on that there were, in fact, two sets of steps of recovery. The first is practical and is made up of the steps described in chapter 8 – the actions members are advised to take in order to resolve their problems. The second set described above, deals largely with inward changes. We noticed that as members take these steps they begin to change and take on board qualities such as honesty, humility and proper pride. They probably do not realize it, but, when they deal properly with their problems, they cannot help but change themselves. The steps are spiritual although they have to be taken by practical means. There is a point when members see that the Recovery Programme describes experiences they have been enjoying, up to a point, for some time. This may explain why the steps are written in the past tense.

Stage 1, re-orientation, is covered by steps 1 to 3. Consider step 1 – whenever it is taken, on a member's first night or later, it is taken implicitly. They do not, at the time, put their finger on these words and subscribe to them. Rather, they accept that they must stop gambling and do whatever is necessary to get themselves out of trouble. It may actually be some time before they think through the implications of this and fully appreciate the words of this first step. But, when they are able to do this their reason for following the programme becomes more obvious to them and more inspiring.

The words of steps 2 and 3 present difficulties for some members as we shall see in chapter 15. They may not be sure of the Power.

Even so, progress is impossible unless members actually believe that their lives can change. They also have to exercise their will and make decisions about the direction their lives will take. Later the words of the steps may haunt them as they realize the normal way of thinking and living has more to offer than they supposed. If so, even before they find their own understanding of the Power, even if they never find that understanding they will be on stage 3, probably even while they are still engaged on stage 2.

Stage 2 is expressed in steps 4, 5, 8 and 9, but it does not exhaust their meaning. For instance, stage 2 has a strictly financial inventory. Even so, as recovering compulsive gamblers renew their relationship with their families and meet and settle with their creditors, they recognize some faults in themselves though they do not yet record them in an inventory. When they realize that it is of fundamental importance to deal with their defects of character, not just repair the damage they cause, they will be on stage 3.

In the same way, as they settle down with their families and pay their creditors they will become aware of deeper and more serious ways in which they have harmed others. When they see that this is what matters most they will be on stage 3. They will also find that making such amends is harder even than budgeting and paying debts. This progress will show in their therapies. One man spoke often of his middle child – he had destroyed the natural confidence she should have had in his love. It took a few years of agonizing effort to restore it.

Not everyone, however, consciously and fully, enters upon stage 3. Some do not even get the best out of stage 2. One man expressed concern that he might gamble again when his debts were clear. At that time, for him, that was the end of the road.

The goal is normal life and generally, *normal* is understood as meaning the average, the usual, the expected or what is generally required. Members of Gamblers Anonymous who complete stage 2 in the sense of restoring essential relationships, paying debts, recovering their basic personality and regaining their self-respect may, in this sense of the word, be said to be normal. They can pass in a crowd. This achievement should not be underrated and many are more than satisfied with it. Some who leave at that stage after two or three years fall back into gambling but there is no reason to believe that all of them do. If they integrate back into the general community it gives them all the more chance to make further progress in the personal quality of their lives.

There is, however, another interpretation of the *norm*, which is more idealistic. It refers to a standard that someone aims to achieve, and a proper way to be – this is what stage 3 of the programme is all about. Those who have the best chance of experiencing stage 3 appear to be people who continue to attend Gamblers Anonymous meetings long after they have paid their debts. There is a necessity for a desire to change and improve character and personality. To some this seems to come naturally, although obviously a great amount of effort is still required.

Others find it more difficult to change their ways. They are able to cope with giving up gambling but it distresses them that at home and elsewhere they are still as disagreeable and as difficult to live with as they were when they were following their old way of life. This may be a legacy from childhood. Perhaps they were taught to be tough and self-sufficient by friends or members of their family. This does not mean that they are strangers to kindness and gentleness, but because any behaviour like this was always despised as softness when they were younger, they are inhibited from showing their true feelings. For the same reason, while they may feel love, they may find it difficult even to say the word, let alone show their true feelings. They make no secret of this though and seek all the advice and help they can get. Most make progress because of their strong desire to do so but it is usually a slow process and the amount of effort required is tremendous.

Among those who are the most disadvantaged in this respect are the child gamblers we considered in chapter 12. Serious involvement with gambling interferes with their adolescence. When they should be learning to interact with others they start to become increasingly solitary and self-regarding. When they should be starting to face up to the facts of life they are confining themselves to their dream world instead. As a result these children, as adults, have a lot more to make up for than lost schooling and lost career opportunities.

Some 'defects of character' disappear as you start to correct relationships with other people. Others are less easy to rid yourself of but it can certainly help if you tell those whose lives are affected by your shortcomings that you know your faults exist and that you are trying to correct them. It is, in any case, important to admit these things to another person. If you make the confession to yourself alone you will only succeed in passing the information from one pocket of your mind to another without doing anything about it.

When you begin to make amends to the people you have hurt in the past, you may still be thinking about yourself rather than about them, still using them, just as you did when you were gambling.

Take heed of the warning in the programme of the danger of hurting
them all over again. Try to consider their feelings and put them first.
Don't just use them as a means of getting something off your conscience. The person you have hurt may well have forgotten all about
it. Alternatively they may not wish to have the matter brought up
again. In other cases a simple but sincere apology may be enough,
however, if you have seriously damaged your relationship with them
and feel that you need to do more to make amends, it will be up
to you to find the best way to do it for them – not an easy task.

Step 10 explains the choice of title for this chapter. The continuous process refers to the personal inventory which you will have
to continue taking for as long as you live. This will involve you in
observing and being sensitive to other people's reactions so that they
become the mirror in which you will be able to see yourself. Slight
gestures, brief changes of expression or tones of voice, will tell you
when you have offended. You will then be able to reflect upon
whether it was your attitude or something which you said or did that
caused the offence. Once you have identified what is wrong, you can
apologize and try to improve your performance. In this way you can
continue to re-mould your character.

Of course the third stage of recovery requires a way no less than
the second. The basis for this is provided in the GA handbook which
includes *a definition of a mature person* and *My daily moral inventory*.
The latter contrasts liabilities with assets, for example: 'Watch for
self-pity and strive for self-forgetfulness.' Most commonly used and
most valued is: 'Just for today', which reads as follows:

Just for today I will try to live through this day only, and not
tackle my whole life problem at once. I can do something for
twelve hours that would appall me if I felt I had to keep it up for
a lifetime.

Just for today I will be happy. This assumes to be true what
Abraham Lincoln said, that; 'Most folks are as happy as they make
up their minds to be.'

Just for today I will adjust myself to what is, and not try to adjust
everything to my own desires. I will take my luck as it comes and
fit myself to it.

Just for today I will try to strengthen my mind. I will study. I will
learn something useful. I will not be a mental loafer. I will read
something that requires effort, thought and concentration.

Just for today I will exercise my soul in three ways: I will do somebody a good turn, and not get found out; if anybody knows of it, it will not count. I will do at least two things I don't want to do, just for exercise. I will not show anyone that my feelings are hurt; they may be hurt, but today I will not show it.

Just for today I will be agreeable. I will look as well as I can, dress becomingly, talk low, act courteously, criticize not one bit, not find fault with anything, and not try to improve or regulate anybody except myself.

Just for today I will have a programme. I may not follow it exactly, but I will have it. I will save myself from two pests: hurry and indecision.

Just for today I will have a quiet half-hour all by myself and relax. During this half-hour, sometime, I will try and get a better perspective of my life.

Just for today I will be unafraid. Especially I will not be afraid to enjoy what is beautiful, and to believe that as I give to the world, so the world will give to me.

Just for today I will not gamble.

Although this programme does not constitute a practical way it does help members of Gamblers Anonymous and Gam-Anon to see what they must do, to form resolutions and to carry them out. It is the kind of guidance they need as they venture back into everyday life.

Step 12 has to be considered as, above all, a step of recovery. It is often one of the first to be taken. I have seen a member sharing with a new arrival all the wisdom he had learned in one long, full gambling-free week. I have no doubt that this did more than anything else to consolidate his new way of life. Indeed, those who do twelfth step work always get a lot out of it. They realize how much progress they have already made. As a result they become more confident that they will succeed in their own recovery. Furthermore, because they have to make the effort to understand other people's situations, their capacity to care widens and deepens.

Using the telephone to talk to new members after their first meeting, to keep in touch with each other between meetings, to enquire how friends are getting on when they have missed a meeting or two, is all part of step 12. They may also take a turn at being 'on call' volunteering to accept GA and Gam-Anon calls in their own

homes so that they can share the work of helping with enquiries.
Alternatively they may provide support for those members who are
involved in trying to set up a new group and who need help from
members of the parent group until the new one is established and
is attracting new members of its own.

Some make taking the twelfth step almost a way of life, for several
years. When asked what drives them they usually say that they want
to put back some of what they have taken out. They want to *spread
the message* and know that the basic qualification for doing so is to
assimilate it and to visibly live it themselves so that at each meeting
the new members are given fresh hope that they too can make a
recovery and can live a fuller and more rewarding life. Some of these
people are wonderful leaders and have burned like beacons of hope,
others have been great rocks of strength.

We must be sorry, but we should not be surprised that only a
minority of members becomes fully involved in twelfth step work.
Although members come, first and foremost, for themselves, they
soon realize that they depend upon the others. But they start to
make real progress only when they recognize that the others also depend on them. The signs are even more encouraging when they start
trying to play their part in doing something about this.

Perhaps something more is needed in helping to create the way
along which stage 3 may be trod. Maybe it would help if there were
some goals to aim at. These might be expressed as questions such as
Am I becoming more considerate of others? Am I a responsible person? Am I reliable? Each of these words, considerate, responsible and
reliable, could head its own moral inventory. To be sure, success
must be noted and recorded. The longer members are in Gamblers
Anonymous, the more their therapies should be concerned with the
present rather than with the past. They could ask themselves: 'What
incident has shown me during this past week that I am still too in-
considerate, irresponsible or unreliable and what should I do about
it?' The complementary question would also be valuable: 'What incident showed me and my family (or colleagues or friends) that I am
becoming more considerate, responsible or reliable?'

This is not an excuse for self-indulgence. It has to do with being
sensitive to others and of being aware of our effect on them. It is a
slow and painful business. It requires great self-discipline. It is all a
part of the effort to adjust oneself to what *is* and this does not come
easily to those who have for years tried to adjust everything to their
own desires. However, it is worth the effort because as members succeed in this, they and those around them begin to lead happier and

more productive lives and the ripples of success spread out and touch every member of the Gamblers Anonymous group they attend.

Recovery, for members of Gamblers Anonymous and Gam-Anon alike, must begin with practical actions. Wrongs must be put right.

Although they may not be aware of it, as recovering gamblers perform these practical actions, their attitudes to life begin to change. They become nicer and better people.

Indeed, by the time their debts are clear and they have restored basic relationships, they will be 'ordinary' or 'normal' people. At that point many are satisfied and leave the fellowship.

Others continue to attend, to complete what they see as unfinished business. They enjoy feeling 'clean' and alive but they are aware that they still have character and personality defects, resulting from their past lives, with which they must deal if they are to be truly happy, co-operative and useful.

This leads them to explore the 12 steps of the recovery programme more closely and deeply. It helps them grasp and explore the inward meaning of the practical actions which got them out of trouble.

It helps them see the need for a moral, as well as financial inventory if they are properly to make amends to all the people they have harmed.

This pursuit constitutes the third stage of recovery.

For three reasons at least it does not lead to priggishness. First, the depths to which gambling led them cannot be forgotten. Second, their gratitude for their new life increases. Third, they want to improve as people so that they can enjoy other people more and in turn be enjoyed by them.

15

The 'Power' of our own understanding

Finally it is necessary to consider the references, in the Gamblers Anonymous Recovery Programme (which also apply to Gam-Anon), to the God and to the Power of our own understanding. Those words may give the impression that Gamblers Anonymous is a religious society. The handbook makes it clear that it is not:

> *GA is composed of people from many religious faiths along with agnostics and atheists. Since membership in GA requires no particular religious belief as a condition of membership, it cannot be described as a religious society.*

The statement continues:

> *The GA Recovery Programme is based on an acceptance of certain spiritual values but the individual member is free to interpret these principles as he chooses.*

The meaning of the word spiritual, as used by Gamblers Anonymous, is defined as follows:

> *Simply stated, the word can be said to describe that characteristic of the human mind which is marked by the highest and finest qualities, such as generosity, honesty, tolerance and humility. Inasmuch as the GA fellowship advocates acceptance of these principles as a way of life, it can thus be said that GA is a spiritual fellowship.*

In this context, the word 'God' cannot have its usual theological meaning. Even so, it is enough to prevent some convinced atheists and agnostics from joining and to provide others with difficulties for as long as they remain in it. Those who have a religious affiliation naturally interpret the word in the light of their own faith but find that the new experience they have found in Gamblers Anonymous or Gam-Anon gives that faith new life and meaning.

If a new member asks what these words, 'Power' and 'God', mean, he is, in effect, advised to wait and see. Waiting clearly helps because, after perhaps a year or so, even members who have no formal religious leanings whatsoever, say that the words are beginning to evoke a response from them. The words have begun to associate themselves with one or more aspects of their experience in the group. Quite often the Power is associated, either more loosely or more closely, with the group. That is understandable because the importance of unity is felt to be fundamental. (The Gamblers Anonymous Unity Programme is given at the end of this book.) My concern here is to describe, as well as I can, the way in which experience in Gamblers Anonymous or Gam-Anon can give meaning to the words 'Power' and 'God'.

The steps in the recovery programme in which these words appear are:

2 Came to believe that a Power greater than ourselves could restore us to a normal way of thinking and living.

3 Made a decision to turn our will and our lives over to the care of this Power of our own understanding.

7 Humbly ask God (of our own understanding) to remove our shortcomings.

11 Sought through prayer and meditation to improve our conscious contact with God as we understand Him, praying only for knowledge of His will for us and the power to carry that out.

The experience which GA members go through usually arouses wonder, even awe. Members never feel that what is happening is commonplace. When they are trying to explain it to an interested outsider they sometimes put it like this: 'Miracles can be performed at once; the impossible takes a little longer!' These words show that for them a space had opened up in which they might find the God of their own understanding. Another member trying to define these experiences, united everyone at his meeting one evening when he said: 'There is power in the room and you can feel it.' That sense of an anonymous, even impersonal, power for many gives added significance to the words of step 2. The speaker and many others in the room had begun to return to a normal way of thinking and living

HV6710 N3 P3. 1986

Hee-Jean chung

E, mail : H7777C@AOL.Com

but they were not sure how they had done it. What they had achieved seemed to them to be little short of a miracle so they began to accept the idea that they truly had been helped by an external force of some sort – as though they had been carried by the tide or blown along by a following wind.

Much the same considerations can be said to apply to step 7. Why, after having said in the previous step, 'Were entirely ready to have these defects of character removed' can we not simply say, 'And decided to remove them' in step 7? It is necessary to take this decision, otherwise, without the effort that follows it nothing will change. But the formulation of such a decision is as much like a prayer as a resolve – the task which gamblers attempting to recover face is formidable and the defects of character are deeply ingrained.

The experiences ex-gamblers have at this stage are, of course, intensely personal. For this reason, when members discuss them they usually refer to 'my power' and 'your power' instead of saying literally 'the power of my (or your) own understanding'. All these things are shared by agnostics, atheists, religious believers and others who hold no firm views, alike. Perhaps for that reason people do not refer, in the same way, to 'my God' or 'your God'. Any one of them, though, when describing how, in the previous week, they have succeeded where they might have been expected to fail, may talk of a 'miracle' and associate it with their Higher Power.

Those people who are still attending GA after five years may be assumed to be attempting continuous personality and character change and most if not all of them will know very much what they mean by the Power or God of their own understanding.

The step which gives most help to those who are happy with the concept of the God of their own understanding and the greatest difficulty to those who are not, is step 11. If we read it again in the light of what has been said above we may understand why.

> 11 Sought through prayer and meditation to improve our conscious contact with God as we understand Him, praying only for knowledge of His will for us and the power to carry that out.

If there is conscious contact with God and if He has a will for us, we are moving beyond the experience of winds and tides and unknown influences towards belief in God in the religious sense. I can understand that that would trouble some people and I would like to help them if I can.

Let us begin with the word meditation and ask what we do when we practise it, religious believers, agnostics and atheists alike. We consider the ideals we hold and the principles we accept as objectively as possible. At the same time we reflect on our lives as they are. We try to bring those ideals and principles into closer contact with our way of life so that it may be more influenced by them. We do not do this to feel the glow of a halo or to improve our reputations. We do it because we are responding to the invitation offered to us by life to enjoy the best existence possible. The invitation is a conditional one because our true acceptance of it depends on our willingness to obey certain moral and physical laws. So, if and when we meditate, what we do is to review our own life in the light of what we consider to be the purpose and meaning of life generally. Put another way, this means facing up to Life's moral and physical ultimatums.

Beyond Life there is, for some, the God of their own understanding (and in truth no one can go beyond that) who is, for them, Life's meaning and also its fulfilment and interpreter. Religious humanists go that one step beyond agnostic and atheist humanists but up to that point all share the same challenge, sense of adventure, and discovery.

I once spoke about this issue in a workshop devoted to the consideration of the steps of recovery at a Gamblers Anonymous convention. Afterwards, one man who had been struggling to accept the references to 'God' and the 'Power' for years, said that from that point on *Life* was going to be his Higher Power. He, and others like him, seem to experience no fundamental difficulty in recognizing a higher power. They know the place it fills in their life. All they need is to be able to call it by a name which they can honestly accept. In Gamblers Anonymous at least, the question must always be left open as to whether the experience that underlies this is of God or is alternatively one of drawing on hitherto untapped human resources.

Step 3 which deals with the turning of wills and lives over to a Power recalled for me the difficulties I experienced as a boy and as a young man. In Church, along with others, I was often urged to give myself – my life, my affections, my energies – to God. I was given to understand that this should be a complete, decisive and once-and-for-all dedication. I was ready to do it and when an opportunity arose I tried my best but the end result was always the same. I could never convince myself that such an absolute decision had been made. I just couldn't see how it was possible to package your life and hand it to God and, if you were able to, would you *know* that you had done it? As time went on the pressure left me but I never found the answer to these questions.

Some years later, when I became involved with Gamblers Anonymous and discovered that there were people attending the meetings who could accept the words of step 3 without any worries or objections, I asked myself why they too were not afflicted with my problem. I eventually came to the conclusion that it was because they were more concerned with experience than with words. By this I do not mean to imply that they were careless with words. Rather, I believe, they pressed on with the actual dedication that was essential to their recovery and took what meaning they could from the words as and when they needed it. They re-orientated their lives in stage 1, they followed the way in stage 2 and they pursued character and personality change in stage 3. Because their new life demanded that they care for others, bore their responsibilities and told the truth, they gave themselves wholeheartedly to a thorough performance of those things.

If awareness of a Power of their own understanding, greater than themselves, is going to dawn for them, it will do so while they are engaged in this struggle. If and when it dawns, their awareness of that Power will be associated with their efforts to achieve the new way of thinking and living to which they are being restored. As they give themselves up to pursuing the new way, so they are giving their will and their lives to that Power. So I saw it and realized that for some time past I had seen it, but not so clearly.

There is a sense in which what we desire, what we aim at, is already there, as a possibility, just waiting to be realized. If you telephone Gamblers Anonymous, Gam-Anon, Parents of Young Gamblers or any of the other kindred fellowships, there is the invitation to: 'Come to GA and your problems will be over'. You will have to come to the meetings, you will have to re-orientate your life, you will have to follow the way and make the necessary character and personality changes, *but it is all there now, waiting for you to claim, if you can rise to the challenge.*

Remember, *you can win* provided you take the decision, and make the effort required, the odds *are* on the side of recovery. Those who know this know the Power of their own understanding.

The Recovery Programme includes two references to God and two to a Power, in each case to be interpreted as 'of your own understanding'.

At the same time the handbook points out that Gamblers Anonymous is not a religious society.

Even so the very presence of these words seems enough to keep away some atheists and agnostics.

The Power is really a matter of one's own experience, which they associate with the Power they feel exists in the room or the group. People often talk of 'miracles' of achievement. For some the group is the Power. For others the Power is God as 'He' is conceived in their own religious association. There seems to be an unknown quantity involved in the experience. Gamblers Anonymous has a 'spell' which can break the 'spell' of gambling and hold people on the road to recovery. This 'spell' is felt by atheists, agnostics and religious believers alike. No one would want to lessen its effectiveness by defining it too narrowly.

Epilogue: Having read all this what can you do?

That depends on who you are.

If you have recognized either that you are a problem gambler or that you have one in the family, I hope you have already begun to do what you now know you have to do. I wish you well.

If you are a member of the caring professions and have stayed with me until now I think I can assume that the book made sense to you. I hope it will help you to recognize and assist those among your patients or clients who are problem gamblers or are involved with and affected by one. If that is true I expect you will have asked for literature and advice from Gamblers Anonymous, Gam-Anon or Parents of Young Gamblers, whichever is relevant. Local groups of Gamblers Anonymous and Gam-Anon would welcome your request for an invitation to an Open Meeting. Such contact would be helpful for both you and them. I hope that, in co-operation with your colleagues you will try to find additional ways of helping those who do not succeed in Gamblers Anonymous.

If you are a general reader I hope you will try to help others understand that problem gambling, like problem drinking and some other conditions is tantamount to an illness, so that those who are directly and indirectly affected may feel encouraged to seek help and not be discouraged by the stigma which is at present attached to their situations.

If you are a member of Gamblers Anonymous or Gam-Anon you will know that I wish you well. Here and there things I have said may have raised your eyebrows. If so, I hope you will not just reject a thought because it is new, but allow time to consider it. Though I have been a member of the fellowship I have been able to look at the experience from the outside and that, with long years of reflection, provides another perspective which, I hope, can be helpful to those who are involved with the problem. Finally my thanks to all of you for teaching me so much about gambling and even more about life and the God of my own understanding. I have written this just after the twenty-fifth anniversary celebrations of Gamblers Anonymous in the UK and, thinking back over the years I am grateful that all the hundreds of lives which have been saved in that time were not left to go to waste.

The Gamblers Anonymous Unity Programme

Unity is the most precious quality our society possesses. Our lives and the lives of all to come depend squarely upon it. Yet unity in GA cannot automatically sustain itself. Like personal recovery it demands honesty, open-mindedness and, above all, vigilance. In the words of Benjamin Franklin: 'We must hang together, or assuredly we shall all hang separately.' So there can be no sacrifice too great if it will strengthen our essential unity. In maintaining unity we have begun to traditionally practise the following principles:

1 Our common welfare should come first; personal recovery depends upon GA unity.

2 Our leaders are but trusted servants; they do not govern.

3 The only requirement for GA membership is the desire to stop gambling.

4 Each group should be self-governing except in matters affecting other groups or GA as a whole.

5 GA has but one primary purpose – to carry its message to the compulsive gambler who still suffers.

6 GA ought never endorse, finance or lend the GA name to any related facility or outside enterprise, lest problems of money, property and prestige divert us from our primary purpose.

7 Every GA group ought to be fully self-supporting, declining outside contributions.

8 Gamblers Anonymous should remain forever non-professional, but our service centres may employ special workers.

9 GA, as such, ought never be organized; but we may create service boards or committees directly responsible to those they serve.

10 GA has no opinion on outside issues; hence the GA name ought never be drawn into public controversy.

11 Our public relations policy is based on attraction rather than promotion; we always need to maintain personal anonymity at the level of press, radio, films and television.

12 Anonymity is the spiritual foundation of the Unity programme, ever reminding us to place principles before personalities.

Further Reading

Robert Custer, M.D., and Harry Milton, *When Luck Runs Out: Help for Compulsive Gamblers and their Families*, Facts on File Publications, New York, 1985.

William R. Eadington (Ed.), *The Gambling Studies: Proceedings of the Sixth National Conference on Gambling and Risk Taking*, Bureau of Business Administration, University of Nevada, Reno, NV 89557-0016, 1988.

For publications of the Australian National Association for Gambling Studies apply to: Dr Mark Dickerson, PO Box 2486, Canberra, ACT 2600.

For those who wish to make an academic study of the subject the following books are recommended:

Dickerson, M.G., *Compulsive Gamblers*, Longman, London, 1984. A balanced survey of scientific theory and research to 1982.

Galski, T. (Ed.), *The Handbook of Pathological Gambling*, Charles C. Thomas, Springfield, Illinois.

Lesieur, H.R., *The Chase: The Career of a Compulsive Gambler*, Schenkman, Cambridge, Massachusetts, 1984.

Ross, G., *Stung: The Incredible Obsession of Brian Moloney*, Stoddart, Toronto.
The story of a compulsive gambler who embezzled $10 million from the largest Canadian bank.

For a proper appreciation of the state of current research it is essential to read recent volumes of the *Journal of Gambling Behaviour*, Human Science Press, New York.

Other important scientific papers appear from time to time in the following journals:

British Journal of Addictions
American Journal of Psychiatry
Addictive Behaviours
International Journal of Addictions
British Journal of Psychology

Useful Contacts

UK

Gamblers Anonymous/Gam-Anon
17–23 Blantyre Street, London SW10 0DT
(01 352 3060, 021 233 1335, 061 273 3574, 0742 25596, 041 445 115 or 0272 329367)

Parents of Young Gamblers
(021 633 4771 daytime)
(021 443 2609 evening)

AUSTRALIA

Gamblers Anonymous/Gam-Anon
Level 2, The Wesley Centre, 210 Pitt Street, Sydney, NSW

Gamblers Anonymous/Gam-Anon
St Luke's Anglican Church, Dorcus Street, South Melbourne, Victoria

USA

Gamblers Anonymous/Gam-Anon
National Service Office, PO Box 17173, Los Angeles, CA 90017
(213 386 8789)

Gamblers Anonymous/Gam-Anon
Eastern Regional Information Center
PO Box 135, New York, NY 10016